Squashed Possums

Off the beaten track in New Zealand

Jonathan Tindale

This book is a work of non-fiction (mostly).
To be precise, the author has estimated it to be 98%
non-fiction (probably) with a margin of error of 3% (more
or less). This raises the curious and unsettling possibility
that the book may be anywhere between 95% and 101%
non-fiction. Confused? I know I am. So, to summarise,
this book has taken a few liberties with what is considered
the truth, and yet, may be so honest it might have bent
reality out of place by one per cent.

Names, characters, places and incidents are real,
except when they are the product of the author's
imagination and may be entirely fictitious. Some names
have been changed to protect the individuals identity.
The caravan's experiences are, more or less, the author's
own recollections that have been lent to the caravan.

Edited by Chloe Marshall
Cover design by Gavin Dupée

For Amy

"The essence of the lone caravan is that it was 'alone' - away from society, a place where domestic proprieties could be scoffed at."

The Caravan by Jock Philips

"Early British settlers to Australia were amused by the number of Aboriginal place names with repeated syllables. The Britishers made up the word woop-woops as a satirical mock-native word, making fun of some of the existing native place names. New Zealanders soon adopted the word, using it to mean a place so distant that it has no real name, instead pronouncing it with shorter vowels as wop-wops."

Curious Kiwi Words by Max Cryer

Contents

Introduction

Let me be honest with you, I do not know who wrote this book. A few weeks ago, a package arrived at my home. A brown jiffy bag. There was no return address. No explanation as to who, or what, had sent this to me. Inside, was a thick wad of loosely typed papers. The pages were a little worse for wear, and worn around the edges with a faint whiff of the country. As I sat down to read, I was even more shocked by the words that jumped out of the wrangled pages.

More than a decade ago, I had lived in a caravan in New Zealand. It was what the locals referred to as a lone caravan, a ramshackle place in the middle of nowhere, so far removed from suburban life that it had no address. This was the wop-wops, only to be found by traversing a long and winding dirt track, rutted with hazards and holes. For several months, I had made this strange place my home. I grew to both love and, at times, hate this place. But I cannot deny the extraordinary effect it had upon me, and upon the contents of this mysterious book.

The package reveals an account of my life in this place. From the moment I reversed off the edge of a cliff and almost tumbled into the oblivion, to my close encounter with a possum, it's all there. The long nights enveloped in darkness, with nothing but the stars for company and how, for a moment, the experience turned my head inside out.

On the subject of mind altering experiences, not only has someone else written my story, but they've also used extracts from my diary. How the author came by it, I cannot say, but another narrator is involved and this voice is definitely not mine. And who is it that shares their account of such a strange tale? None other than the caravan itself.

God damn! What madness is this, you ask. Yes, you heard me right. The narrator of this book is none other than the caravan. Or so it appears. I cannot comment on the provenance of the author. After all, I received this book anonymously. But before you get wrapped up in wondering how a vehicle could perform such a feat, let me tell you that this is a vehicle with a story to tell.

This lone caravan it is one of the last of its kind. It is iconic in its own quiet, unassuming way. There are books and photographic galleries dedicated to it. To the casual observer, it is an eyesore, a large heap of junk waiting to be swept away and replaced by something cleaner and more comfortable. Yet this place is a prominent pointer to the country's past, a time when pioneers lived on the fringe of civilisation and endured the elements without any modern conveniences. Brave and resourceful souls found ingenious ways to construct what they needed from scraps of wire and metal, lessons that have been learnt and passed on to this very day.

This is the story of one such solitary caravan; a tale about life in a wild, untamed place in contrast to the rest of the modern world. New Zealand has always been a remote place, with strange and unique wildlife that has evolved through the protection of thousands of miles of sea from the nearest predator. New Zealand was the last significant land in the world to be colonised by people. Polynesian explorers arrived some eight hundred years ago and many centuries later, the Europeans made their discovery. The collision of these two peoples continues to reverberate to this day, as the country deftly balances accusations and reconciliation thanks to the Treaty of Waitangi.

More than a century and a half after the Treaty, New Zealand has grown to a modest population of 4 million. You don't have to travel far to lose yourself in an isolated place. The country's cities and towns are dwarfed by the vast swathes of forest and wilderness. So, perhaps this book is not so strange after all; for who better to tell the tale of remote New Zealand than the lone caravan itself.

Chapter 1

Not just
a caravan

I'll bet you ten bucks you've never read a travel book like this before. A travel book written by a caravan? A lone van out in the wild? I wasn't always an inanimate object. I know a thing or two about travelling. I have been hitched to the back of many a vehicle and pulled all the way from the Pacific Isles of Northland, down to the bleak township of Invercargill in the south. But no longer. We all have to retire someplace and here I am, a simple wagon perched on a small scenic hill far from the nearest town, in a place sometimes romantically and a little cryptically referred to as the 'wop wops'.

Hang on, have I misled you already? I am not just a caravan. Let me offer you my dimensions. I am two caravans, one smaller, one larger, connected by a short umbilical corridor. As you can imagine I am not as mobile as I once was. My wheels have long since been removed and replaced with short stumps of tree trunk. I'll admit, at first it was embarrassing. Whoever heard of a caravan without wheels? But I learned to live with the ignominy. What choice did I have? At least I don't have to worry about getting a puncture and falling over.

Above me stands a slanted corrugated metal roof that valiantly attempts to protect me from the elements. It's not a thing of beauty it must be said, but it keeps me dry. The rain bounces off it with a rat-a-tat-tat like the trigger happy gunfire in a Rambo movie. My roof is held in place by several wooden beams that plunge vertically and diagonally all around me. You might say they embrace me and hold me together.

Of my two caravans, the smaller one contains a simple kitchen, furnished with a pantry of spices and a temperamental fridge. There's no oven. Instead there's a camping stove with two electric hobs, and a microwave that might pre-date the Apollo missions. A small laminated formica table has seen better days, and is beginning to peel around the edges. Outside, sat on my tow cable sits a loud, clumsy washing machine that shakes and clatters whenever it's used. Trust me, it's an earthquake trapped in a white metal box.

My second van is a larger model, with panoramic windows from the bedroom through to the library. Whoever is staying with me can hardly complain about the view. There is an epic vista of forested hills and the grass is startlingly green. At night, the light of the Milky Way pours through my windows, our spiral galaxy as effective as a thousand 100 watt bulbs.

A small iron stove stands next to the double bed. Slapped on the chimney is a yellow post-it note that reads: 'Do not use!' The rusting chimney was blocked some time ago, and has not since been fixed. The useless stove is a constant reminder to any tenant that when winter approaches, my central heating is not so much inadequate as non-existent.

I did mention a library, but I'm no stately home, so don't get any far fetched ideas. There's little room to spare, but an entire wall is chocka with shelves and these shelves are stuffed with books. The contents make for an eclectic literary time capsule. A weathered volume of Brecht and Chomsky paperbacks stand beside the well-thumbed poems of Hafiz. The great Sufi master sits next to the collected works of Shakespeare. I absorb information when I can, reading over the shoulder of whoever is staying with me at the time. The radio is a pleasant distraction, but I have no such luxuries as a television, hot running water, internet or even a bathroom.

I do have a bath though. A bath in a caravan? Well, sort of. Let me explain. On the edge of a nearby stream, or ditch rather, stands a typical household ceramic white tub that's currently half full of dead leaves and green stains. If you're so inclined you can fill the bath from a hot water hose, or with a bucket of ominously green and cold stream water. The stream mostly consists of slimy algae, which isn't an appealing prospect I must say. I wouldn't be too impressed if someone tried to wash me with frog flavoured ditchwater...

Those of you paying attention may have noticed that I didn't mention a toilet. Well, I don't have one. But my tenant doesn't have to make like a bear and bury his business in the woods each day. Instead, there's a small building with a gas powered shower and hot water about five minutes walk away. Each call of nature requires a head long scramble down an almost vertical slope, only to meet the pine forest and trudge through the thick, pine needle strewn undergrowth. You have to traverse the hill like a, what do you call them, oh I remember, a slalom skier, a few steps left and a few steps right, cautiously sliding your way down. And yes, I have seen more than a few visitors slip and fall face first into a tree.

You have the measure of me, but I ought to introduce you to my latest resident. Jon is a young bloke, still in his twenties and standing a frustrating half inch below six feet tall. I'll tell you now for nothing that he's bound to bump his head on my door frame a few times, before he remembers to duck. He seems to have temporarily replaced Anne, who lived with me these past few years and then mysteriously packed her bags and left last week. We'd been together long enough that she'd learned to adapt and adjust to living here in the wild woods, but Jon looks more than a little lost. He's got a lot to learn, to really understand what it takes to live in the wop-wops.

This story isn't just the tale of a lonely van, but of this young man's life here. I don't try to imagine what is going through his head. I am not a psychic caravan. I leave that to the Romany caravans and their shiny crystal balls. Jon keeps a journal and every night he scribbles away in his erratic scrawl. I am not ashamed to admit that I intrude on his privacy and read over his shoulder from time to time. After all, there's no telly so what else is a van to do for entertainment? I don't think he'd mind if I shared the occasional diary entry with you. After all, this is his story too.

Saturday 1 March

What had I done? What is this place? I'm not sure if my jaw dropped, but my stomach certainly lurched sideways as I faced these strange surroundings. I actually felt nauseous. The truth of what I'd done finally dawned on me. When I'd planned to come here it seemed like an adventure, moving to this peculiar and distant caravan in the hills of New Zealand. I'd seen photos on email from the comfort of my own home in London, but nothing could quite prepare me for how rustic it was. No, not rustic, but primitive. Like a pioneer's wood cabin, far removed from society, a place of almost absolute solitude. How on earth they'd ever managed to move the vans up this hill was a complete mystery. Looking around, I realised that I'm surrounded by forests, and not even the slightest sign of human life. I had no idea where the middle of nowhere was, but it looks like I'd not only found it, but I'd made it my home.

   Getting to my new home was no simple task. On first arriving, I'd been collected from the nearest town, Paraparaumu, by my neighbour

Jean. She collected me in a beaten up white Mazda and we quickly left town, crossing the train tracks and heading for the hills. The Maungakotukutuku road is a zig zag route with hairpin bends that cling to the side of the vertigo inducing valley. To our left a steep hill rose above us. To our right, a sheer vertical drop revealed itself with the road plunging into the distant forests below. Climbing up the valley, the road reached level ground and the tarmac soon turned into gravel. The Mazda bounced along the dusty unsealed track, giving off clouds of dust as it flew across the uneven slippery surface. My first feeling was absolute shock, followed by a dash of wonder and a great deal of near terror. Where on earth were we going? I'm clumsy by nature and I was none too confident about driving to my new home everyday without calamity.

What bright idea had brought me here exactly? Well, I'd exchanged my one bed flat in suburban west London for a caravan in the New Zealand bush. I'd also swapped working for the government with working as a librarian in the small town of Paraparaumu. Living in a van might sound a bit desperate, but I'd decidedly rejected a comfortable life in favour of my solitary home in the woods. Other exchange offers had included a woman who had contacted me from Hamilton, further north towards Auckland. She'd offered me the use of her comfortable suburban four bedroom house, and was even willing to throw in her husband as part of the package. She figured that her other half could keep me company while she's away, which struck me as odd to say the least. Unsurprisingly, a spell in surburbia complete with a househusband was not the slightest bit appealing. Other opportunities came in from the Australian outback, Canadian British Colombia – where the nearest neighbour appeared to be a bear, and a sunny spot near Bondi Beach in Sydney. I turned them all down in favour of living in the bush. Madness? Perhaps. But as soon as the photos of the rag tag lone caravan appeared in my inbox, I was hooked.

Reflecting on my primitive new home, I tried to remind myself why I was doing this. My intention at first had been simple enough. Escape. Working as a civil servant in London, I recall the feeling of restlessness in my job. I'd started to feel like a cog in the machine, staring into a PC screen all day long, tired of reminding myself that this was better than working in an asbestos factory or gutting fish for a living.

One month before I left London and chaos was all around. It was February 2003. London was preparing for a terrorist attack and the impending war with Iraq had left everyone nervous. The newspapers were filled with threats of poison gas being pumped into the London Underground or even a rocket attack over Heathrow. There was a palpable tension in the air. Only two weeks before my departure, I had returned home from work, shoes caked in snow, after another painfully slow journey battling through London's paralysed tube, train and road network. Kicking my shoes off, I'd put on the kettle, sat down, switched on the television and watched a documentary simulating a radioactive dirty bomb at Trafalgar Square, promptly devastating central London, not a hundred yards from my office. Perhaps moving twelve thousand miles to a remote caravan in the woods wasn't such a bad idea after all?

But if I'm honest, there was always more to this than escape. After all, I hadn't met many people who'd willingly swap the comforts of their own home for what was essentially a hut in the woods. I'd always felt a connection to wild places, and as a child I had whiled away many a carefree hour swinging across rivers on rope swings. I have fond memories of my father building a shelter in the woods, using nothing but branches and vines. It was great fun enacting the Arthur Ransome and Enid Blyton stories that my mother had read to me, and far more exciting than the troubles of school. But playing in a forest for an hour or two before returning to my home comforts and loving family was quite a contrast to moving to a forest, some twelve thousand miles away.

End of diary entry

Chapter 2

Feathers and furry things

A small plump hedgehog flies overhead. A surreal sight I'll admit, but I'm more worried that Jon might crash his car straight into me. He'd certainly never seen a flying hedgehog before, and I wish he'd look where he's going when he's behind the wheel and headed straight for a helpless stationary vehicle. "Holy Christ" I heard as he skidded to a halt, blinking and rubbing his eyes. A falcon flew gracefully past. Held in its talons is a small passenger, most likely his in-flight meal. The hedgehog's little feet dangle in the air, wiggling frantically as the bird of prey swoops gracefully overhead. Rising triumphantly through the valley, I reckon it's a one way ticket for Mrs Tiggy-Winkle.

It is March 2003, and it's a cracker of a day - we're having one of the hottest summers on record in New Zealand. I'm sure I've got a barometer somewhere, but I find the radio a more reliable source of information. Tarmac is melting on the roads and the trains are struggling to run - the wrong kind of heat, I suppose. Personally, I find the extreme heat is less of an issue when some bugger has pinched your wheels and there's nowhere to hurry to. Luckily the nearby pine trees and my rickety roof offer enough shade to stop my walls bleaching in the midday sun.

Jon is settling in nicely, and seems to think that he's living in a holiday resort. For the moment at least, he's lost the worried expression that seemed like a permanent fixture ever since he arrived. I think it took him all of three minutes to unpack and move in. There's a handful of t-shirts, some other old clothes and a few CDs, that's about it. He seems happy enough as he drags a chair outside to admire the view, wiping the sweat from his face. He's even found a length of washing line, tying one end to my roof and the other to a protruding tree root. Hanging up a sheet, he finds relief in an impromptu sun guard as he kicks off his shoes to enjoy the grass beneath his feet and admire the view. And what a view it is. I am sat on top of a hill, a clearing covered in lush green tussock grass, stretching to the vast pine woodland. Beyond lays a cool river concealed by aged mountains of dense indigenous forest. Rolling clouds scud by while the rabbits bounce about, their long ears twitching to every tweet and whistle of the local birdlife. It's sweet as.

The sun sets, eclipsed by the surrounding hills, and the rabbits vanish from view. Our only company is a New Zealand native owl, the morepork. His wide bulbous eyes that carefully track his prey are not be seen, nor his graceful and silent movement. He's a nocturnal bird that's sensitive to light so he's not the easiest of creatures to spot, but he makes his presence known through his yelping call. "More pork" he demands, like a rude customer in a restaurant. The Maori consider the high pitched, piercing yelp to be an ominous forewarning, and they aren't wrong. We would have uninvited visitors before the night was over.

BOOM! BADAMN! BOOM! Jon is rudely awoken from a deep sleep by a series of loud thumps pounding my roof. He'd fallen asleep listening to the Iraqi war coverage and I suspect the poor boy thought he was under attack from Patriot missiles. BOOM! Scratch, scratch, scratch. Then it goes quiet again. Jon steps out of bed, reaches for the torch and throws some clothes on. He gingerly peers outside and takes small, careful steps into the darkness, peering over my roof with a dim flash of torchlight. He really ought to get some new batteries.

"Argh!" he yelps, before stepping back so quickly that he almost falls and rolls down the hill. Nose to nose with a possum, the creature peers back at him through the darkness. Jon is slack jawed at meeting this visitor. The possum is rather less impressed and clings to a wooden beam supporting my roof as if I were a branch. I interpret the possum's mousy expression as 'this is my forest, what the hell are you doing here?' The creature is illuminated by the torchlight with an eerie glow, with the sort of face that only a mother could love. You'd never describe a possum as cute - they're rather large, meaty creatures. Their bodies are almost pear shaped and they're grey and furry with a face like a rodent on steroids, complete with a big bushy tail.

They're buggers, possums. That's a bit harsh, you might think but I have my reasons. They defecate on my roof. Their claws are like razors, and this particular visitor will leave me with a permanent scar no doubt. My reasons may be personal, but possums are also responsible for eating much of New Zealand's forest and consequently decimating the indigenous wildlife. There are about 30 million possums in New Zealand, meaning that there's almost eight possums for every one person.

I hear them as they munch through around nine thousand tonnes of leaves, berries and fruit every night. They were imported from Australia where ironically, they're protected. I like Australia - it's not short of open space and the Ozzies appreciate a good home on wheels. Many of their trees have defences such as spines, prickles or poisonous leaves – plus Aussie possums have predators. But here in New Zealand possums have no natural enemy, and their numbers have swollen. Not only do they eat the homes of native birds, they will also eat their eggs and chicks too. The buggers have even been known to push kiwis out of their burrows, simply for a dry place to sleep. And if they get inside a van, you're a gonner. Years ago when I was sat in a caravan park near the Coromandel, a possum sneaked through an open window of a neighbour and shredded every single inch of carpet, curtain and furnishings within. The van was destroyed in about ten minutes flat, and the owners promptly dragged it to the nearest scrap heap. It was a messy way to go, so I'm relieved that Jon had the sense to shut the door behind him when he stepped outside this evening.

This particular possum is transfixed by the torchlight, his ears twitching. Their call is a blood-curdling scream, said to resemble the sound of a woman being brutally murdered, chilling the bones of those who are unfamiliar with this harrowing noise. What with their murderous cry, razor sharp claws and wide array of victims the possum resembles an extra from a horror movie - the bastard child of Freddy Krueger and a fat squirrel.

New Zealanders are a resourceful bunch, with some pretty imaginative uses for the pests. I've been overtaken by motorcyclists in the South Island with live possums stuffed down their jackets to keep them warm, with furry noses peaking from between their jacket buttons. But being used as living insulation isn't the worst fate for a possum. People aren't squeamish about killing animals in New Zealand, particularly vermin that devastates the natural wildlife. Back in the day, my wheels have rolled with a bounce and a thud over a possum or three. You can even buy novelty squashed possum shaped chocolates, complete with instructions on how customers with a sweet tooth should "pursue, knock down, and flatten any possum that you have the opportunity to kill."

Friday 21 March

My close encounter with the possum was quite the awakening, and it wasn't long until I found myself in the ziggurat obsessed art deco town of Napier in Opossum World. Essentially just a shop with a startling array of possum related products, this is the closest thing that New Zealand has to a possum theme park. On offer are warm gloves and socks, shelves of teddy bears, and even kinky handcuffs, all proudly made from the hides of possums. The macabre possum museum section, resembling a Victorian freak show, was particularly odd with shelves of stuffed moth-eaten possums leering unpleasantly from behind their glass enclosure. If Dr Frankenstein had been a taxidermist from New Zealand, this is what he'd have created.

A slot machine with an attached plastic rifle encouraged visitors to take bloodthirsty pot shots at the possums while avoiding the native birds, as they bob about among the artificial undergrowth and trees. My favourite feature is a Mini embedded in the wall, with a squashed possum flattened beneath a rear tyre. Possum road kill is a frequent sight in all but the most urban areas of New Zealand, and as an added comedy touch, standing on the roof of this vehicle was a choir of possums, each holding a little song sheet. A red button flickered invitingly in front of me. Upon pressing the button, the furry quartet squeaked a lively "On the road again…" like a macabre version of Disney's singing chipmunks, Chip an' Dale.

Returning to the caravan that night I fell asleep listening to the horrific scream of many rampant possums. I was grateful I'd had the presence of mind not to watch the recent movie sensation, The Blair Witch Project, before moving here. A film about a group of students running around an unknown dark forest, being hunted and killed by some unseen malicious force was not a memory that I wanted to be fresh in my mind. My new home is not a place I'd want to succumb to an

attack of the heebie-jeebies. My imagination
is active enough, without the thought of
murderous witches and terrified victims
stumbling around and screaming like a pack
of wild possums.

End of diary entry

I worry about Jon - the forest at night can be an inhospitable
place. He's not lived in the wild of the boohai before and I've
seen how a man's imagination can run away with him when
he is alone in the dark, night after night. I suspect it won't
be long before he'll be talking to himself and mumbling like
a madman, or worse, talking to me. I have plenty to say, and
I'm a real chatterbox. But despite being the narrator, I'm
still just a caravan and I don't possess any vocal facilities.
Don't be thinking I'm a talking van - that would be foolish.

Actually, I am not the first van whose thoughts made it to
print. I might be unusual, but I'm not unique. I met an old
1963 VW campervan some time ago. It had a red and white
paint job, nicely restored after some lunatic had given him a
thorough muralling many moons ago. You could still make
out the outline of the round peace symbol though. The van's
name was Urge and he'd been around the block so many
times it was a wonder his axle hadn't snapped.

Truth is, Urge was a little funny. Kept muttering that
he'd been responsible for one of the great American
counter culture novels, Divine Right's Trip. But he was
pissed because his story had been hijacked by some bloke
called Gurney Norman, who'd apparently taken all the
credit. Urge was alright, as VW vans go. I find them a bit
up themselves personally. These days, their owners usually
have deep pockets. The vans are spoilt rotten, with their new
re-upholstering and every sprocket and part painstakingly
restored. I used to consider myself lucky if my tire pressure
was checked. No-one so much as offered me a new coat of

paint. Perhaps I should be more grateful... Caravanners can be a strange bunch of folk. I've seen more than a few fellow vehicles decked out like a psychedelic explosion in a paint factory. The vans weren't too impressed with their appearance, and neither was I.

Whump! Jon sat bolt upright. "What was that?" he said to himself. Thump! There it was again. Distracted by the noise, he turned down the radio, put down his notebook and peered outside into the darkness. I don't know what he expected. Some angry possum flinging projectiles at me? Nope. Every year near summer's end, the local insect life retreat to the warmest, brightest place they can find in the inky dark night. Fat furry-winged demons fling themselves at my panoramic windows like suicide bombers. For a few nights my artificial illuminations transform me into a botanical insect house, albeit inside out. My exterior is crowded deep with thousands of little legs, tiny wings, and all manner of bugs and creepy crawlies. The night is endlessly black, and the insects are drawn to me like moths to a flame.

One particularly mischievous bug managed to penetrate my defences, giving Jon one hell of a fright. In fairness, its vibrating wings buzz so loudly they might be mistaken for the rotor blades of an Apache helicopter. Things were about to get a little Apocalypse Now for one bug in particular. Jon rolls up a newspaper, leaps over a chair and swats the tiger moth, almost the size of a small bird, with a swift right hook. Splat! The moth smears along the inside of my window - I really wish people would take more care.

Jon tunes into the radio for a little human contact. The news is dominated by the long anticipated invasion of Iraq. "Targets of opportunity...fires rage in Baghdad...we will disarm Iraq and free its people!" a voice proclaims. This is the world's first fully televised war, or so the radio says. We wouldn't know, I haven't had a television in years. The distant violence is giving me a real sad on, and I'm relieved when Jon turns the dial from the sounds of missiles and explosions to a local programme about New Zealand's wildlife.

"Long before the Earth's continents had taken on their current appearance, even before the extinction of the dinosaurs, the country that was to become New Zealand had already been torn loose. Isolated for millions of years, we became a great biblical ark," explained the pompous presenter. Maybe I've spent too long in this forest, but it seems like New Zealand has always been some kind of global version of the wop-wops, lost and remote in the Pacific. "There were no mammals so instead of animals two by two, birds would take their place, producing a unique and slightly bizarre set of flightless characters including kiwis, wekas and the world's only flightless parrot, the kakapo."

New Zealand didn't remain undisturbed. When people first arrived here some eight hundred years ago, the local wildlife had a mighty shock. It turns out, squashing animals has been a national past time in this country for an awful long time. First on the scene were the Polynesian explorers, who would become the Maori people. They arrived in a land of abundance. For over five hundred years, they hunted and gobbled up a vast array of unique bird life, including varieties of coot, wren, geese and swans - now all lost. The birds simply didn't know how to defend themselves and because they'd forgotten how to fly, they were unable to escape. Good grief! The poor chooks must have wondered what had hit them: "Oooh, I've not met you before. I wonder if you want to be my friend." Thump! Sizzle! Gobble! Indigenous birdlife made for several hundred years of tasty meals, and some thirty two species were dispatched before the Europeans even arrived. If the local tweeters and flappers thought that things couldn't get any worse, they were in for a very nasty surprise indeed.

Do you remember all those mammals and predators that our birds never had to worry about for millions of years? Well, the Europeans set up what they called acclimatisation societies, with the sole purpose of adapting New Zealand to their home lands. Salmon, trout, red deer, frogs, swans, possums and rabbits were all introduced. Our local chooks simply could not cope with the new competition. Many more species died due to the loss of their habitat, along with the addition of predators and disease. Our native birds were incapable of adapting to their new environment, so they never stood a chance. One poignant example was the flightless kiore bird who, driven to the edge of extinction, was surviving on the remote outpost of Stewart Island. Then the lighthouse keeper arrived with his pet cat and that, as they say with a meow and a chomp-chomp, was the end of that.

The radio was almost morbidly apocalyptic in the story it told, but the good news is that there are survivors. The most famous of all is the country's national icon - the one and only kiwi bird. Now, this patch of wop-wops might be a remote place, but even here there's little in the way of hospitality for a kiwi. After all, possums pretty much fall from the trees like apples in an orchard. I have a certain empathy for these odd, elusive creatures. As a munted old caravan in the wild, I suppose I'm an oddity too. Since I can't provide a little shelter for a kiwi bird myself, I will have to live a little vicariously through Jon who is lucky enough to lay eyes on one.

Saturday 22 March

If I spent too much time at home, the walls closed in on me. It's a small space that reminded me of a hobbit hole, which is well and good if you're four feet tall with hairy feet. But I found it so poky that I bashed my head on the ceiling if I moved too quickly. Sometimes, the only answer was to get out for a while.

So, I turned the ignition on the Mazda and tentatively navigated the car along the winding switchback road. I was quickly brought to an abrupt halt as ahead, stood a white fluffy roadblock of sheep. Four or five of them were nonchalantly assembled in the middle of the road. My arrival put them in a sudden panic as they turned tail and trotted down the road, and with that I followed slowly in pursuit, herding them along the road until they eventually veered right through a hole in the hedge. One after another they disappeared, until the last sheep panicked and bolted for the gate. Unfortunately for him, the gate was firmly closed and trotting at full pelt he bounced dramatically and was almost catapulted back the way he came. I'm sure, for a moment, that he looked surprised - if such an expression is possible in a sheep.

I was searching for more exotic wildlife than New Zealand's ubiquitous sheep. The closest place to see a kiwi bird is in the neighbouring town of Waikanae, at the Nga Manu Nature Reserve. This small patch of land is full of local wildlife and native trees, all fiercely protected by a powerful electric fence. Enclosed within these defences is the reclusive North Island brown kiwi - housed in a large, darkened room with an abundance of tree roots and leaves, like a Howard Hughes of the natural world.

On first inspection, the kiwi was careful and slow, concentrating on his feeding. He disappeared for long periods into his nest box. A small monitor showed grainy black and white CCTV footage from inside the nest, but he was hard to spot and pretty well concealed. The water sprinklers were flicked on and the kiwi burst into life, rushing out from his nest into the rain, suddenly sprinting about manically. "Is he supposed to run around like that?" enquired a local family on a day out, incredulous to see their national icon with such energy and movement. Running in circles and figures of eight around the tree trunks, the kiwi was having the time of his life. The conservationist who had switched on the sprinklers explained: "He loves the rain like you wouldn't believe, but his partner, she hates it. She'll hide in her nest until we switch off the sprinkler."

He's an eccentric character, the kiwi. He's as round as a football, and furry rather than feathery with an outlandishly long beak and a pair of thick stumpy feet. He reminds me of Groucho Marx, I think they have the same lopsided waddle. Unfortunately the kiwi bird is grappling for its very survival. Maori refer to them as "te manu huna a Tane", the hidden bird of Tane, God of the Forest. The kiwis' ability to hide in the remotest corners of the country ensured its survival and almost proved its downfall. Thanks to these exemplary hiding techniques, the elusive creature was fast disappearing from its native habitat before anyone had the chance to notice.

Unlike any other bird, the kiwi has nostrils at the end of its beak which are used to forage and scent out grubs, enabling the bird to fill the gap in the food chain left by the absence of native mammals in New Zealand. This curious creature was used to foraging about slowly, snuffling with its long beak, looking for worms. He stood a foot tall, when he wasn't leaning on his beak like an old man with a walking stick. His head bobbed up and down and his wings were noticeably atrophied through the course of evolution. Stomping about with his massive, oversize comical feet the kiwi has managed to survive quite against the odds. A recent nature documentary had shown a mother kiwi defending her young from a stoat. To the nation's amazement the mother kiwi had leapt into the air, successfully kicking the aggressor out of her nest using her size ten feet. The public had reacted with equal amounts of shock and respect - everyone knew that this was an unusual bird, but nobody ever suspected that the kiwi was a champion kick-boxer. My heart warmed to the kiwi immediately, and I couldn't help but be impressed that such an unlikely misfit of a creature could be chosen by New Zealanders as their national icon.

End of diary entry

You may not find a kiwi bird here, but you're never far from the wildlife in these woods. Again, the peace is interrupted by a loud scratchy noise coming from my kitchen ceiling. Jon is spooked and investigates me quizzically, exploring my shelves and roof with care in case something might jump out and bite his nose. He rests his hand on my ceiling as if checking a pulse - I suspect he wonders if I am alive, imagining himself sitting inside a beast like Jonah in the whale. After all, the gentle rhythmic breeze outside could easily be mistaken for inhaling and exhaling.

I do hope he doesn't give me a name. Many think they have the measure of me, indeed one lonely middle aged man I knew as Smelly Bob named me Karen. Karen - Karavan, get it? He'd spent too long with his budgies. Damn things dropped pellets of guano all over my nice formica table. I was a Christopher for a while too, after some God loving family likened me to the patron saint of travellers. And who am I now? What do you call an isolated lone caravan on a hill, am I a nervous antisocial Derek, or a scary lone woodsman like Billy Bob? Neither option appeals.

I digress. Jon discovers the source of the noise, namely the tufts of dead grass sticking through an open air vent. I know that this vegetation mound is a nest, but I'm unable to tell him. Besides, it would spoil my fun. So, Jon visits our neighbours for advice. Not the emu farm, the other neighbours. "I think the local wildlife are moving in, what do I do?" he asks Andrew and Jean. They aren't more than a few minutes walk away, but a small hill maintained our privacy. It was Andrew who had arranged for my relocation from a small caravan park to this remote spot on the hill. He looks like he's born for country life, stocky and red faced. A shoe-in for the 'Least likely to succeed as a management consultant award, 1989'. Surprisingly, he used to be a merchant banker, though you'd never know from his appearance. Like me, he is a retired traveller and in the past he'd commuted the vast distance between Auckland and Brisbane. And like me, he now lives in one hundred and sixty-five acres of solitude, filled with hard wood eucalyptus and pine trees. He earns a crust while working from home, designing security platforms for internet sites. "I rarely leave the place now," Andrew, the virtual hermit, explains with a shrug. "Jean gets the shopping, and I have everything I need here." Jon can't help but ask "When was the last time you left the wop-wops?" and Andrew isn't too sure, "A few weeks now... or is it a few months?"

I like Andrew, he's a dag with a mischievous sense of humour and he has a little fun with Jon. "Your neighbours, the emus, well one time, one of them escaped from the farm and fled into the bush," he grins, raising his eyebrows. "It was days before they found it, running wild." Andrew hands Jon a box of poison. "I'm not sure" Jon says, nervous of what he might end up killing. "Well, it's probably rats, and you don't want to be living with vermin."

This was how, within a few weeks of arriving in the bush, Jon made his first kill. The poison works by dehydration, so the rodents made for the nearest river and died there rather than leaving their rotten corpses festering in my roof. Jon was changing and adapting to outdoor life. He'd drawn the line - the wildlife would remain outdoors, for the moment at least.

One of the hardest things about living in the bush if you're not used to it, I'd say, is the silence. Trust me, it was a shock coming here. I'd been accustomed to the constant clatter of life on the road, or parked up amongst the chatter of a caravan park. If all you've known is the constant buzz of towns and cities, this place can take some getting used to. There's no passing traffic, no voices from any neighbours, no aircraft flying overhead and no hum from electric pylons. Nothing. The only sound is the gentle rustle of the leaves in the breeze. I could tell the isolation was getting to Jon. He'd twitch whenever a noise broke the silence. A crack of a twig or a strong gust of wind rattling my doors would set him off, pacing about my floor, restless and unsettled.

Jon found refuge in the radio. Alas, the local broadcasts can make for dismal listening. A selection of easy listening ballads introduced by a local DJ as "More hits from the 50s, 60s, 70s and 80s..." Describing the songs as hits is pushing it a bit, and someone should sue the radio stations for misleading their audience. I don't recall ever hearing any Elvis Presley, Beatles, Chuck Berry, T-Rex, or Duran Duran. Instead, almost every radio station broadcasts an unrelenting and brain-rotting parade of one-hit wonders and easy listening records. The radio stations seem to have acquired their playlist by trawling charity shops, only to discover that all the decent records were scratched and worn out, so instead they stocked up on obscure Perry Como and Connie Francis albums. New Zealand has a keen recycling policy which is to be commended, but these records ought to have been melted down long ago. The commercials provide some form of respite though, as a jolly female voice offers a range of buns, baguettes and ciabatta from her café, only to be followed by a Carry-on inspired advert for an establishment called Big Joe's garage. "Situated on the corner of Dickson Street and Cockspur Avenue, hehehe!" It was as if Carry On favourite Sid James had never died and instead retired to New Zealand, earning beer money for recording innuendo laden adverts.

I'm partial to a tune or two. I might not have ears, but the frequencies resonate rather pleasantly through my walls. My most musical visitor is of the feathered variety, and his name is Tui. He is a most unusual bird - one of those creatures that's often mentioned in wildlife documentaries. They have the rare ability to not only mimic the song of other birds, but to also produce a realistic impression of a camera. Tui often sits in the branches overhead, happily warbling his clicks, whirrs and hiccups. And when he gets in his zone he can beep, buzz and almost beatbox for long stretches of time. In some inspired moments he sounds like Star Wars' R2-D2 reading Tolstoy's War and Peace. He's a natural entertainer. His jet black plumage and tuft of white feathers around his neck gives the impression that he's dressed in a dinner jacket with a napkin tucked into his shirt. It isn't difficult to see why New Zealand's music awards are named the Tui's.

Jon typically spends the evening cross-legged on the bed, writing his thoughts down in his journal. He prepares himself a simple supper, boiling a bag of ready-made ravioli. His attempts at cooking aren't up to much, but then I don't have much of a kitchen, so who am I to criticize?

Outside, it's still insect season and I can feel some 786 little legs flitting about on my windows. I'm not sure if it tickles or itches, but it's a curious sensation. One fat beetle scuttles across the pages of Jon's book. Snap! He is squashed instantly with a sharp slam of the covers. Ouch. Bad karma.

Another intruder. A finch flies through the kitchen door. I'm reminded of the budgies all over again, and I'm worried that the distressed bird will excavate the contents of his interior all over my interior. He swoops through my cramped confines, panicking but just about managing to avoid bouncing off my walls. Jon springs into action and in the absence of a net, lays a hand on a sieve and takes chase on a frenetic pursuit. The bird takes refuge by swooping behind the microwave, scuttling and flapping about in a frenzy before pausing to catch its breath. Jon heaves the microwave off of the fridge with a cough and a sneeze. One swift lunge later and the sieve captures the wheezing bird, who is taken outdoors and relaunched into the air. The little bird is quickly joined by his partner who'd evidently been waiting in the nearby branches. Better out than in, I say.

Saturday 12 April

The forests of New Zealand are a hostile environment for most of the country's indigenous wildlife. If you want to turn the clock back to see these creatures in their natural habitat, then you need to visit New Zealand's outlying islands.

Islands are often a fertile haven for unique wildlife; Madagascar has the lemurs, Mauritius had the dodo, Jurassic Park had dinosaurs and New Zealand's islands are no exception. They're not easy to reach and for good reason - the more people visiting these places, the greater the risk of something dangerous being introduced to these small pockets of surviving birds. I was fortunate to find myself on a boat headed out to the savage triangle carved out of the horizon on the Tasman Sea - Kapiti Island.

Kapiti Island is a prominent local landmark. Every day, I'd spot this jagged mountainous outcrop of rock. There's a particularly good vantage point on the road home, where I'd pull over on occasion to admire the view. Once, I'd parked the car to admire the sunset, as the sky shifted from the dramatic hues of blood red into a rippled crystal blue. The sun set dramatically behind Kapiti Island, it was a spectacular view and a perfect moment. Well, almost. The experience was only slightly marred by a discarded Big Mac polystyrene box and a used condom dumped on the grass verge... remarkable what they give away with Happy Meals these days, isn't it?

On a sunny day without a cloud in the sky, our group boarded a small boat and bounced across the strait to Kapiti Island. With some surprise our bags and pockets were thoroughly searched before boarding the vessel. "Overdoing it a bit aren't you?" I asked as my day-pack was thoroughly rummaged. Kapiti Island's security arrangements are tighter than LA airport. "Sorry mate," came the reply, "but it took us years to rid the island of predators, and if anyone was to smuggle a pair of stoats back here, it would be catastrophic for the wildlife." Seems hard to imagine that anyone would deliberately attempt such a thing, yet only recently the alarm had been raised when a letter was received at the office of the local newspaper, claiming that possums had been re-introduced to Kapiti Island. The Department of Conservation (DoC) had meticulously searched the island, before coming to the conclusion that the message had been a vicious hoax and since then, they've promptly upped security. While international customs ransack bags for explosive and illegal drugs, the DoC search for possums, stoats and rats. Don't underestimate the DoC though, they manage about 30% of the entire country. If the kindly conservationists, geologists and ornithologists that comprise the DoC's staff ever decide to overthrow the government and take over the country, as unlikely as that sounds, they'd already have a pretty decent head start.

A rum old sea dog with a white wispy beard and a passionate hatred of possums met us at the pebbled beach of Kapiti Island. "Imagine how much vegetation it takes to feed thirty million possums every day. Buggers! Everyone one of 'em. Our kiwis are now all but gone from the mainland." He continued: "Even a few years ago there were enough wekas that they were still considered a pest, rummaging through peoples garbage cans, but now they're endangered as well." A pair of wekas scampered about our attentive group, the round flightless birds nosing for food with their long beaks. We're told that wekas are scavengers by trade and not naturally aggressive, but that doesn't prevent one weka from using his beak to defend itself from my trouser leg. "Ye better watch ye bags, those wekas are devious buggers and they'll unzip a backpack and have anything edible or shiny before you know it!" The Department of Conservation might manage the island, but the birds had made it quite clear who runs the show.

To protect the habitats of endangered birds and the Maori burial grounds, much of Kapiti Island remains out-of-bounds to the public and prying sightseers. With a choice of only two paths available to the public on the island, the coastal route, and the track leading to the peak, we opted for the latter. Following the path through the bush, we paused to watch the friendly fantails as they flitted through the undergrowth, displaying their tail feathers. An unwieldy wood pigeon landed heavily on a branch that's clearly several sizes too small for him. Realising his mistake, the pigeon frantically thumped his wings, returning his vast weight to the air before the branch split under his weight. The primeval forest is filled with a humming chorus of bird songs, sounds that not so long ago would have filled every valley and plain of New Zealand. The view from the peak was spectacular. Marlborough Sounds lay hazily to the south across the Cook Strait, small islands scattered along the waters with Kapiti Coast to the east. I shuffled to the edge and look straight down the west face of the island, a sheer vertical cliff plummets dramatically five hundred metres into the turbulent sea below. Hungry from our walk, we cracked open a picnic of ham and cheese rolls, while defending our lunch from the locals. One devious weka strutted around our small circle, stalking us like some small descendent of the velociraptor. His head bobbed up and down with curiosity as he eyed us hungrily.

Walking the return journey, a kaka followed, the inquisitive green parrot swooping from branch to branch before climbing down the tree trunks using his beak as a third claw. He stopped a few feet ahead and obligingly posed for the camera, watching us expectantly. He's no fool. The bird seemed to be deliberately putting on this little performance for an edible reward. As bird brains go, the kaka is second only to the crow. Kakas have been known to unscrew jam jars using their talons and beak. Perhaps the kaka and the weka ought to form some sort of criminal alliance. The kaka could get the visitors' attention by performing for scraps, while the weka ransacks their backpacks for snacks and valuables. I certainly wouldn't put it past them.

A group of fellow walkers stopped abruptly, staring into the forest. "What are you all looking at?" I asked. A lady with a floppy sun hat was poised with her SLR pointed into the bush. "Look, there's a takahe," as she pointed excitedly towards a rather portly bird with green and blue plumage and a bright red beak, sitting in the tussock grass. Standing in quiet awe, we observed the bird snuffling around, looking for insects.

The takahe is one of the most extraordinary creatures in New Zealand, if for no other reason than the fact that in 1930 the takahe was presumed extinct. The only place you'd find a takahe was stuffed and mounted in a museum case. But a determined amateur naturalist, Dr Geoffrey Orbell, was quietly fascinated by these birds and after many years of diligently searching in his spare time, he rediscovered the takahe in November 1948. A colony of 250 birds had somehow continued to survive, finding refuge in the wop-wops in the unexplored and remote mountains of Fiordland.

I stood there, quietly watching this phoenix from the ashes, as the takahe clambered closer and closer, my camera discreetly clicking away. A figure approached from the distance, walked down the path, shouting at the top of her voice "Mike! What you up to Mike?" I was appalled - what was she doing? Was she some inconsiderate visitor who had foolishly mislaid her hen-pecked husband? Didn't she realise that she'd scare away this elusive creature?

To my utter amazement, instead of running away scared, the takahe skipped and hopped towards the woman, as fast as his little feet could carry him. As the woman approached I realised that she works on the island for the DoC, and is calling out to the takahe. Scampering around her feet, Mike the takahe darts between her footsteps like a love-struck puppy, proving that you can find love in the most unlikely of places.

End of diary entry

There is more to New Zealand's wildlife than birds and possums, but since my wheels were replaced with tree stumps, my view of the sea and opportunity to spot dolphins is rather limited. But there was a time when I'd pass through Kaikoura, where marine life is so plentiful that you could skim a pebble from the water's edge and hit a seal, a dusky dolphin or even a humpback whale.

I was rather fond of another caravan. She sold grilled crayfish. Nin's Bin was her name. Nice curves, with a decent lick of paint on her, but it's hard to have a relationship when you're always on the move with little control over your destiny. I was a reliable van and I didn't often break down, but I'd blow a puncture as I was approaching Nin's Bin. People took me to Kaikoura so that they could boat out to the whales and scuba with the dolphins, but I was very aware that if I was to swim with the dolphins then I'd be a one way trip to Submarine Town. Once, I did consider unhooking myself and sliding down the cliff to see what things look like from the inside of the big wet, but I don't think I'm sturdy enough to be a coral reef.

I'm more of an aviary than a fish tank, although there's one bird I'm not sorry to see the back of - parrots. There are three flavours of New Zealand bush parrot that I'm familiar with. There's the kakapo, who I have no axe to grind with, as he's like the dodo of Kiwi birdlife. As John Cleese once said, he's a dead parrot, except he isn't dead. Or rather, there are around 100 of these creatures who aren't quite dead. He's not a malicious parrot, not like the others. He's actually a charmingly incompetent creature. The kakapo makes the panda look fortunate, because their chances of mating are even lower. The kakapo mating call is of such a low frequency that prospective partners simply cannot tell where they are, since they produce a deep rumbling noise that you'd normally only get from dub reggae sound systems. That's a parrot I like. Foolish, but without a malicious bone in his body.

On the other hand, the kea and the kaka are terrors. I won't dwell on their subtle differences but the kea lives on the South Island, and the kaka in the North Island. Both are blue and green, and absolute bastards. Oh no, off he goes again, you say, moaning on like he did with the budgies. Well, how would you like it if some feathered monster with a beak like a pair of pliers sat on you, and proceeded to peck and pull the rubber lining from your windows? I've seen them strip a car of all three of its windscreen wipers in under sixty seconds. I saw one land on the shoulder of a small girl in pigtails, peck an avocado sandwich from her hand and swoop into the air with his ill-gotten gains before the unfortunate kid had taken her first bite.

I should be grateful though really. The largest predatory bird in the history of the world was a New Zealander. The Haast eagle once had a mighty wing span of three metres. Their talons were as large as a tiger's and it could dive at eighty kilometres per hour. What they'd have done to a caravan is anyone's guess but they could tear apart the giant moa, a flightless bird that stood twelve foot tall and weighed 500 pounds. I can imagine an impressive battle and if they weren't extinct, these flying tigers would have finished off the emu farm down the road in no time.

Most people accept that the last moa died almost 500 years ago, yet in remote areas of New Zealand, rumours persist that small numbers might still be alive. I was once hauled the length and breadth of the South Island on a moa hunt, looking for these oversize turkeys. My companion at the time, Richard, was convinced they had survived, as the takahe had. We never did find one. Personally, I think they were given a good dodo'ing a long time ago, but Richard kept on believing. He's not the only one either. There's one hotel near Arthur's Pass that made such good business from convincing gullible people there was a lost group of moa nearby, that the owner actually erected a life size statue of the thing.

He had a big brown beard that was thick and dense like a forest. I suspect it was no coincidence that, on meeting him, people often went straight home to mow their lawn. Richard would talk to me as we explored one lonely forest track after another. I've been conversed with more than you'd expect. People prefer people, but they'll bend the ear of their dog or talk to their transport or home, given half the chance. "Caravan," he'd say, "We'll find those giant chooks one of these days, and they'll make a movie about us." The working title was The Mystery of the Missing Moa. He wanted Jonny Depp to play him, which was a bit of a leap if you ask me. On that logic, my part would be played by a Ferrari. A real dreamer, that one. I never complained though. At least he understood how to cruise the roads and the traffic. He used to just go with the flow, rather than constantly jamming on the brakes like some.

His moa obsession had been started by a man called Carl Bjork, who claimed to have seen three small bush moa in the 1940s deep in the lost world of Fiordland. He wasn't the only one to make such claims. In 1949, someone called Miers who worked with the Wildlife Service dug up the scorched remains of a small forest dwelling moa that had been cut with a heavy steel knife - indicating it had been eaten in the last 200 years, some three centuries after it was supposed to have been wiped out. After a great deal of futile searching, the nearest thing to a moa I've seen is a single bone. It looked like exhibit 'A' from a particularly gruesome murder trial. "You could feed an entire family with one of those," Richard pointed out. "One of these birds would have provided enough buckets of Kentucky Fried Moa for several family feasts".

For now, the only oversized wildlife I see is Jon. He seems well settled now as summer draws into autumn. He doesn't leap out of his skin every time the forest creaks or murmurs. He scribbles away at his journal and seems content with the radio for company. He's out most of the day, working at the local library. I've always appreciated a good book myself, and reading what passes through my door keeps me from becoming too restless. Jon comes and goes, but I enjoy his company when he is about, much as people do with pet cats, I suppose. I'm keeping an eye on him though. As I've said before, living in the bush can change a man, play with his mind. Jon hasn't spoken to himself for a while, but I notice he's eating jam straight out of the jar with a spoon. In my book that's an early sign that he's going feral, so I'll be watching him carefully to see how living in the bush may be changing him.

Chapter 3

Pioneering people

The car's headlights flickered ominously. The tranquility of the forest was disturbed by the foreboding echoes of creaking metal. I have to say it didn't look good for Jon. It didn't look good at all. The Mazda shifted and rocked gently on the edge of an abyss. It was night, and there was nothing to see but the headlights of the car swinging gently up and down as it rocked like a pendulum on the edge of a cliff. I shone like a beacon under the headlights, isolated and suspended in space, safe but unreachable as Jon struggled to save himself from falling off the edge. I watched on helplessly, waiting for the crunch and splatter.

That evening had seen the arrival of strong winds and torrential rain. It was a particularly dark night, with the moon and starlight eclipsed by dense cloud. Jon had steered the Mazda through the gate below and pushed into first gear to drive up the last hundred feet of steep slope, as he had done 78 times before. The ground though, was sodden and slippery. He made it half way up the slope before the wheels span helplessly in first gear, absolutely refusing to move forward. Then he made his near fatal mistake. He pulled the stick into reverse, peering blindly through the rear windscreen, hoping to find some traction lower down the slope. Instead, he reversed straight off the track and into the bush, almost falling off the edge of a steep ledge that dropped fifty feet into the forest below.

""*!*!*!* Holy *!*!*dammit!" His profanities shook the forest. He'd opened the driver side door and stepped out of the car. At least, he'd tried to. The problem was, there was nothing to stand on. Opening the driver's door and dipping his foot out into the darkness, he realised that there wasn't anything there. Only an abrupt drop into nothingness. Jon and the car were hanging perilously on a knife edge. Unable to climb out of the driver's side, he pulled the door shut. The small shift in weight caused the vehicle to creak and moan once more. For one awful moment, I expected the car to disappear boot first over the precipice. The Mazda rocked abruptly, as the physics did some quick calculations to decide whether it should stay put, or give into the temptations of gravity and take a short final drop. I've seen The Italian Job and I couldn't help but compare this to the final scene, except Jon didn't have Michael Caine sitting in the backseat, with a pithy: "hang on a minute lads, I've got a great idea."

Jon clambered over the gear-stick, through the passenger-side door, and stumbled out of the car, face first onto the wet grass. Of course, had this been the movies, the car would have fallen impressively over the edge at this moment, but being real life, it didn't. The car simply sat, wobbled and waited.

The following day, the hapless vehicle was towed to safety by a tractor. The short mud soaked track that had already almost proven fatal has since been churned over by the rescue team, and is now utterly puckerood - knackered, you might say. Instead, Jon will have to take a longer route, park at the foot of the hill and climb through the forest to reach me. I don't think Jon quite appreciates how dangerous living in the bush can be. Take for instance the only route to my address, the Maungakotukutuku road. Much of it is little more than a dirt track and it can become a muddy battlefield, with landslides and scattered boulders across its narrow route. A hazardous journey at the best of times, the council's attempts to keep the road clear of debris aren't always appreciated by Jon. Earlier this week, he returned home one afternoon muttering to himself: "What were they thinking - stopping on a blind bend? If I hadn't braked in time, I'd have smashed those workmen's trucks straight down the valley!"

You've noticed that he's talking to himself. I told you so, but I won't dwell on it. What he doesn't realise, is that the Maungakotukutuku's blind bends and low-lying clouds have been a fatal combination in the past. It made the local news. One local bloke drank a few too many beers after a picnic with his family, drove home and rolled the car off the edge of the cliff. Killed everyone. It was a terrible thing. They've since laid tarmac along the most dangerous section, but it only takes one slip of the wheel to achieve a resoundingly final nose thud into some beautiful scenery.

New Zealand's history is filled with adventurous souls, and during the pioneer days more than a few came to a sticky end from crashing their horse and carts or bullock wagons off some cliff and vanishing into the bush. And that's where the similarities between myself and New Zealand's bygone age ended, I thought, until Jon stumbled across an exhibition in the Maori enclave of Porirua.

Sneaking a look at Jon's diary, The Caravan exhibition included a vast array of photography. There were round caravans, square ones, housetrucks, vans painted with murals, sleek Airstreams and even caravans selling hotdogs. Others were in nudist parks, gypsy encampments, homes to hippies and holiday campers. There were showground caravans and suburban caravan parks. And there was the lone caravan...

I am a lone caravan, not one of those who huddles with other vehicles in a dedicated park. To qualify for this select group you have to be in a place away from society -check, far removed from the typical domestic arrangements this brought -check, and typically based in a forest or a remote rural location, such as my own corner of the wop-wops -check.

The lone caravan, according to the exhibition catalogue, is something of a throwback to the European pioneers of the nineteenth century. Well, who'd have thought? Perhaps my great grandparents were their huts and hovels in the bush. You might say the lone caravan is a descendent of the humble shepherds' huts which served as a base for the shepherds whose job was to confine the sheep within the unfenced boundaries of high country runs. They had a curved roof, a simple cast iron stove, a chimney and often wheels. Any home on wheels is a caravan in my book. Throughout New Zealand wheeled huts were used as part of a road train, which carried equipment from one haystack to another. The working mens home on wheels was called a 'stink', hardly flattering but probably appropriate enough after a sweaty day's work. These huts were common enough throughout the 1800s, although if you're lucky enough to see one of these relics today, it'll likely be in pretty rotten shape.

It was a tough life on New Zealand's frontier. There were gold miners and bushmen, hard working, versatile men in a frontier world of back-breaking work. There were trees to be felled, tracks to be made and then of course crops to be planted. You had to be able to light a fire with damp wood, navigate skilfully and travel light. And their home? There were no builders or furniture makers in this new land, so they lived in temporary shelters. A typical pioneer home was known as the tworoom, a kitchen and a parlour consisting of low walls thatched with wood shingles and oiled canvas for walls. They were often isolated, not unlike the motley collection of timber and derelict caravan that made up my own existence.

As a van stranded and put out to pasture, I always thought of myself as alone. Y'know, it hadn't been easy at first, losing my wheels. I didn't know what to do with myself. I'd always been on the move, with different people coming and going. The morning used to come around and I'd wonder where I'd be off to that day. It was some weeks before that feeling of regret ended, and I finally accepted my new vocation. I suppose I'm more social than I thought, but I did adjust and gradually got used to the idea of a sedentary life. In any case, sitting here and slowly rusting sure beats the prospect of being dismembered for spare parts or scrap metal. I suppose you might call it retirement.

I hadn't considered that I was nothing less than the missing link between New Zealand's past and present, a half way house between those hardy pioneers and the soft suburban lifestyle of New Zealanders today. I wasn't just any old caravan, or even two vans bolted together with timber and old scrap. I was a cultural institution, as much a part of the rich fabric that makes this country unique as the All Blacks and chocolate fish (that's fish shaped chocolate, not chocolate flavoured fish by the way).

So, how did I feel about this? Me, a bona fide cultural icon? A van whose reason for being - that is, to travel - was brutally removed when his wheels were replaced with lumps of tree trunk? How do you think I felt? I was the cat that got the canary, or rather the possum that got the kiwi. I would have been unbearably smug if there was anyone to hear. Not bad going for a pile of old caravan... In your face Airstream and your lovely 1950s curves.

If a van in the wop-wops is the modern day pioneers cabin, then what did that make Jon? Maybe he's sharing an experience with the early settlers of New Zealand, and gaining some insight into the life of the noble pioneer. True, his home more closely resembles a hut than a contemporary house, and almost falling off the edge of a cliff into the bush was a typical occupational hazard in days of yore. But he wasn't foraging and hunting for his dinner like many rural men, laying traps and licking his lips from the blood of his latest kill. And he works in the local library, hardly the stuff of pioneering legend. Yet, there are others like him - typically, but not always, men living on the fringe of society. As well as wild caravans, New Zealand has a tradition of loners and it is typically men rather than women who choose to live away from the trappings of society and escape the big smoke.

I have seen a few of these characters close-up in my time. Josh was a part-time loner who liked nothing more than getting away from Mrs Josh. He'd drive me out to some out the way place. Didn't have to be anywhere pretty, for him it was all about what he was getting away from rather than where he was going to. He was a real man, or at least he liked to think so. Never washed, wore the same vest all week and ate cold beans straight from the can. Disgusting, if you ask me. He had a dog, a German Shepherd named Dangerous, but trust me, the pooch was more fifi than fido. Josh would listen to the rugby on the radio and mutter the odd monosyllabic grunt. He wasn't big on words. Instead, he'd sit in stoic silence in his deckchair, smoking roll ups in his pants.

I get to see the most unflattering side of people. You lot behave differently when no one else is about. The inanimate have the dubious privilege of witnessing the behaviour other people don't want you to see... One time, he dropped his smoke and almost set fire to his nebuchadnezzars. Shocking! I've never heard language like it. Then, after a week or so, he'd drive us back to civilisation and expect his wife to do the laundry. This went on, once a year, for six years until he returned home one day to find his missus had gone. She'd left a note explaining that his dinner was in the neighbours cat, his prized record collection was at the local tip and that she had moved to Perth with her new lover Jane who she'd met at the local bottle shop. There might have been a time when a woman put up with this sort of nonsense, but not anymore.

He might be an extreme example, but there's a long literary history of blokes like Josh. Barry Crump's tale of the male world of deer cullers, A Good Keen Man, became a best-seller - although I didn't much care for it. John Mulgan's novel Man Alone sums up a Kiwi man's escape from what he sees as the dull and suffocating restrictions of married and domestic life. The main character, Johnson, spends his time escaping marriage, preferring the simple and undemanding companionship of his mates and his work. I had a battered copy of Jane Mander's Allen Adair, in which the character is on the cusp of wedlock when he observes "He was giving up youth and freedom... this business would fix him, impale him upon the relentless spike of conventional living, take adventure from his life..." He struck me as a selfish and small minded sod. It's fortunate that these writers and characters aren't typical, in the same way that a caravan in the middle of nowhere isn't typical today.

But the man alone, and these drifters and outcasts remain a stubborn part of New Zealand life. Take for instance the Southern Man. New Zealand's most iconic character is no Ned Kelly, Billy the Kid or Robin Hood, one man against the law. Instead he's a loner, one man against society, a blunt yet resourceful character who'd rather spend the day with his herds than with other people. He's not what you might call a new age kinda bloke. Rather, he's a no-nonsense, straight as an arrow typa fella, who loves his pub and drives a ute (that's a utility truck, for all you readers from the northern hemisphere). He's the sort who would never buy a sticky bun with pink icing, even if it was the last one in the shop. He's what the shrinks might call an alpha male and whatever you do, don't tell him that he looks like the cowboy from the Village People. Southern Man doesn't have any time for city folk, and can milk a cow in less time than it takes to say "make mine a decaf latte". He even has his own song:

The Southern Man

Some of the boys,
Got it into their heads,
'Bout movin' up north,
To follow the bread,
That ain't for me,
That kind of thing just don't rate,
This is one Southern Boy,
Who ain't crossin' the strait.

Now I might not be rich,
But I like the things down here,
We got the best looking girls,
And the best damn beer,
So you can keep your Queen City,
With your cocktails and cool,
Give me a beer in a seven,
With the boys shooting pool.

I'm a Southern Man,
Well, I'm southern bred,
I got the south in my blood,
And I'll be here 'til I'm damn well dead.

'Cause here we just know,
What makes a southern boy tick,
And it ain't margaritas,
With some fruit on a stick,
Well it not be fancy,
But when you come from down here,
You know you got the best girl,
And you got the best beer.

Southern Man would have appreciated life in a wild caravan,
as would have Arawata Bill, perhaps the greatest of the New
Zealand pioneers and another lone man. Born in 1835, Bill
was a gold prospector of little success. He explored the most
remote corners of Fiordland in the South Island of New
Zealand, with few possessions except for a billy filled with
cold porridge, and a substantial beard. A caravan would
have been a luxury for Arawata Bill. Yet he was capable
of making the sort of delicious stews that would shame a
professional chef, utilising whatever local birdlife he could
lay his hands on - weka, kakapo, kaka, ducks and pigeons.
He could even muster up a warm meal by carrying hot rocks
from the fire, with a wood pigeon in his saddlebag.

Bill was the son of Irish immigrants, one of many European pioneers that came from the British Isles. Donald Sutherland was another, a Scot who become a sailor before eventually exploring and settling in Milford Sounds. Like many, he was initially drawn to this remote spot in New Zealand's Fiordland in search of gold, but fell in love with the place. He founded what would become the Milford Track, and established its first hotel which is still used to this day.

New Zealand has always appealed to a variety of nationalities and during my travels, my little stove has cooked everything from Korean bimbimbap in Auckland to Polish borscht in Dunedin. I've heard 27 different languages in my time, and I've been sworn at in nine of these. The British Isles might have always been the largest influence yet Dutch and Italian explorers have been here since 1890, as well as immigrants from Scandinavia, especially Sweden and Norway. Charlie Norberg, a Swede, settled down in the outer regions of the Marlborough Sounds. A fisherman and postman, Charlie reputedly knew every rock in the Sounds. He almost came a cropper on Penguin Bay when he was knocked overboard by a wave, while his arm remained jammed in the boat. He was lucky to survive. There were Chinese too, particularly from the Guangdong province, who were drawn by the lure of gold. The first recorded Chinese immigrant to New Zealand was known as Appo Hocton, who jumped ship in Nelson in 1842 and reputedly survived until 1920, to the ripe old age of nearly 100.

That's how New Zealand might have stayed - little more than a scattering of pioneering immigrants, drawn over the centuries from across the globe. But as the sun went down and the autumn breeze blew through the forest and gently rattled my walls, I remember a historian who travelled with me for a while. He was of a mind that New Zealand's isolated communities were wrenched from their lives in the wop-wops by the fateful outbreak of the Great War, and that this war had defined the country and its people.

Together, we used to travel from one small provincial museum to another. He was a meticulous sort of bloke, and he always made sure my tires were good and firm. We got along just fine. We'd arrive at some small town's historical collection and he'd invite the museum volunteers over for tea in 'his' caravan, then proceed to bend their ears until he'd bludgeoned them into agreement. He was the only person I met who was capable of turning a conversation from quantum string theory to Gallipoli. He was remarkable. You mention gerbils, Russian vodka, panel fencing, acrobatics or gerrymandering in Madagascar and he'd shift it back to World War I.

"Y'know mate, in Gallipoli alone, we lost almost three thousand men," he'd explain. He often said the same thing, from one place to the next. "The Anzacs had been transported to Gallipoli for a major assault on the Dardanelles, an operation planned by British First Lord of the Admiralty, Winston Churchill, no less. Anzac and British troops spent eight months in squalid conditions, brutally pinned down by the Turkish Army, as one ill-conceived attack failed after another." He'd pause, for added drama. "The losses were utterly catastrophic. New Zealand suffered a shocking 88 per cent casualty rate. Gallipoli was just the start of it," he'd continue. "Over 100,000 men were conscripted from the North and South Islands, and 17,000 of those were killed and 41,000 wounded. Every region had to contribute a number of men towards the cause, but it was the small rural populations in the South Island who suffered the most. Entire communities were wiped out - it changed the entire country."

He was writing a book about the war, and was determined that young Kiwis didn't forget the sacrifices their predecessors had made. But what surprised and interested me was the role of caravans in The Great War. Caravans were sent from Britain to the frontline, where we were used as mobile units for the Red Cross and as officers' quarters. Field Marshal Haig even sent an urgent request, so his officers could plan on the move while pursuing the retreating enemy. Fifty fellow wheeled homes were sent to the front line in only 48 hours. I don't know how I feel about my kind's role in this great calamity of people. It's not like we have much of a say in things.

The war saw new developments in technology and when the killing was finished, the horse drawn caravan was soon replaced by motorised vehicles. The war was a game changer, for caravans and New Zealanders alike. It was the first time Pakeha (non-Maori) fought alongside Maori rather than against them. Country boys fought alongside their Polynesian brothers, who had learnt to be especially skilful at trench warfare while defending their fortifications from European colonizers. For many Maori and Pakeha, it was the first time they'd even met one another. The Maori Pioneer Battalion even adopted the song It's a long way to Tipperary, to remind them of their homeland:

He roa te wa ki Tipirere,
He tino momao,
He roa te wa ki Tipirere,
He taku kotiro.

E noho Pakitiri,
Hei kona Rehita Koea,
He mamao rawa Tipirere,
Ka tae ahau.

Men who had never left their farms in the Otago were thrown together with Auckland boys. "We ceased to be a couple of islands filled with different immigrants," my historian friend liked to say. "We became a country with a shared experience, bound together by a common loss. Y'know, a lot of this country's problems could be put right, if we remembered that we were all in this together, Maori and Kiwis alike."

Compare these heroic men, individuals and outsiders drawn together by a terrible calamity, to Jon who purchases his cellophane wrapped food from the supermarket. He prefers the pig taken out of his pork, his chicken plucked and his beef thoroughly de-cowed. He wasn't truly a man alone. He was an amateur, a part-timer. But if you want to judge him for not taking his living in the wild seriously, go and watch Werner Herzog's Grizzly Man. Timothy Treadwell and his girlfriend lived in the Katmai National Park in Alaska, before they were killed and eaten by a grizzly bear. Christopher McCandless is another bloke who attempted to live a simple life in the wilderness, and died of starvation after four months. Jon might not be a pioneer but he's no fool. Living here would provide plenty of challenges and hardships, but I can't blame him for not wanting to wind up as possum fodder.

It might sound surprising, considering how beautiful this country's scenery is, but early New Zealanders always had mixed feelings about life in the bush. The Polynesian settlers, they loved the forest, and embraced the abundance of life and food that the New Zealand forests provided. But apparently the early European settlers found the sunless and impenetrable character of the bush rather frightening. They often described it as dark, monotonous and lacking the seasonal variety of European trees. Silent and damp, the woods had few obvious sources of food, along with a constant fear of getting lost. In my experience, the same is still true today. It takes a certain sort of character to appreciate these wild, remote places. Many a time, I remember pulling up at some idyllic retreat for only an hour or so, before being hurriedly towed to some caravan park so my guests could retreat to the familiar company of other people. It was almost as if the forest was something to be feared.

In the past, European settlers had good reason for a fit of the heebeejeebies. In the early 19th century, explorers looking for Maori often noted that they took to the bush.

During the New Zealand wars with the Maori, the woodlands were seen as the preserve of Maori guerrilla fighters. Let's put it this way, the forests were not the sort of place you went with a pack of sandwiches, a flask of tea and a scotch egg. Instead, wiping out the bush and converting it to farmland was part of the process of eradicating the Maori opposition.

It wasn't until the late 19th century that New Zealanders began to have a romantic view of nature, and of wild, untamed environments. Recreational walks such as the Milford Track encouraged a more positive view of the forests as unique and beautiful. Tramping or hiking became a leisure activity, and a network of tracks and huts were built through forested areas, attracting international tourism. From the 1950s, gardeners began to appreciate their native plants. The bush walk became a common recreation, and images of lush vegetation near lakes or on hillsides were promoted to tourists as the beautiful New Zealand that you see today.

Today, Jon and I are in some strange place, not quite in the present but not truly in the past. The age of the pioneers has now passed, but not quite so long ago as you might imagine.

Monday 21 April

I'd been passing through the town of Whakatane when I met Neil. He was a stout sort of fellow - a farmer who owned a herd of cattle in Ohau, east of New Plymouth. He was surprised to hear about my caravan in the outback. "That's rare as hen's teeth these days" he commented. I was quite honest and told him that sometimes it felt like a privilege to live so close to nature, in such a wild and strange place, but that there were also moments when the isolation was hard to bear.

Maybe I was too honest with this stranger, but when you're twelve thousand miles from home and living in a box in a forest, sometimes you just have to talk to someone, anyone. As it turned out, Neil could see where I was coming from and nodded in agreement.

"Hang on a minute," I asked, "you're from Ohau - isn't that just north of the Whanganui National Park?" I'd been hoping to take a trip to see the famous Bridge to Nowhere, which had been abandoned in the forest like some ancient ruin. But the only way to get there was by boat, and the trips had now closed for winter. I'd become quite fascinated by the old Mangapurua settlement, situated a few miles north of Pipiriki. In 1918, returning ex-servicemen were compensated for having survived the Great War and the Battle of Gallipoli, and they were offered a patch of land, deep in what is now the Whanganui National Park. By the 1940's the site had been abandoned, despite the government belatedly building a concrete bridge across the river to improve access to the settlement in 1936.

Mangapurua represented a prominent moment in New Zealand history because this remote outpost of the outback could not be civilised, the wop-wops had succeeded in defeating this last generation of pioneers. The settlement of Mangapurua had been an utter disaster, albeit a heroic one. If only they'd listened to the local Maori, they never would have attempted to live there in the first place. The Whanganui River has a long history of Maori settlement, but in all those years they had never attempted to settle the interior of the vast forest. The rains were too heavy, the forests just too dense. Any attempts to reclaim the land were quickly washed out or overgrown.

Neil had met a few of the surviving Mangapurua settlers, years after they had been forced to leave their land. "One old fella, he said it was the best years of his life. Some of them stayed there for years and years, determined to make a go of it, but in the end, when the government refused to upkeep the road, they had no choice but to abandon the settlement. They'd been through more than we could imagine, but it was the blaady government cost-cutting that done for 'em. No-one realised at the time, but they were all traumatised from shell-shock when they took the riverboat up the Whanganui River to claim that land. This fella had sat next to an old Maori on the riverboat. They'd shared a bottle and the Maori had given him some friendly advice. Warned him not to go. Told him there were taniwha (monsters) living up there..."

Many of these ex-servicemen had lasted as long as twenty years, constantly battling floods and hacking back the ever encroaching forest.   Shell-shocked and lacking the necessary infrastructure, it's a testament to these men that they survived as long as they did, it's a tough life at the best of times. And well before that, the early settlers had survived a long journey by sea, and travelled for months through dense forest before chopping back a slice of land to call their own. But these men had been made of the right stuff, and I felt quite humbled to be having a conversation with someone who

had met the last of these explorers, people
who within living memory had slipped quietly
into the pages of history.

"One occasion, a new settler made his way
by riverboat to the Mangaparua settlement.
Arriving at night, he stumbled through the
bush and knocked on the first door he found,
hoping for somewhere to sleep. The door
opened and a shotgun was poked in his face.
He'd been mistaken for an invading German
army. Blaady hell. Can you imagine that?"

End of diary entry

Before the almighty hosing down that made this hill as
slippery as a bag of wet fish, the ground was baked hard
and the roads turned to dust. New Zealand faced a severe
drought. The last decent drop of water had splashed down
upon my burnt roof several months ago. Truth is, I was
parched.

This corner of the wop-wops is too far from town to
be piped into the main water supply. Instead, I have two
large water tanks collecting rain water. Someone should
bottle and sell New Zealand rainwater. It makes Perrier
taste like old dishwater in comparison. Smooth and fresh,
one can almost taste each of the minerals. And what does
this caravan know of such things? Along with rain water,
I've experienced the spillage of no fewer that 14 brands of
bottled water, 43 bottles of wine, 17 varieties of juice (my
favourite being pomegranate) and urine from 25 different
species. I am a connoisseur of flavours, and a good drop of
rainwater rivals many a Pinot Grigio.

Worryingly, my tanks are dry. I'm tapped out and there's
all but a dribble left. Fortunately Jon doesn't wash very
often and he cleans the dishes in the same water he uses to
cook his pasta. Nevertheless, if it doesn't rain in the next

week or two he'll be forced to arrange for a delivery, but that raises another problem. Could a water tanker navigate the unsealed Maungakotukutuku route without crashing off the winding road, and creating a small reservoir below?

When the rain finally fell, it came thick and fast like a tropical deluge or an act of God. Great fat blobs of crystal clear rainwater ricocheted off my roof in a thunderous drum-roll. The earth drank deeply and thirstily, feeding the glistening plants and half-drained reservoirs. Low lying clouds swept across the surrounding hillside, lending me the appearance of a tree house in a temperate rainforest. All I was missing was the distant chatter of wild monkeys, but the tuis do their best with their eclectic range of clicks and chirrups.

The radio finally announced the end of the water restrictions. "Across the country, gardeners rejoice by watering their prized blooms!" But despite the rainfall, electricity restrictions remained in place, and homes and businesses were still required to reduce their power usage, amid reports of high streets plunged into darkness, forced to switch off all non-essential lights.

All through the following week, rain fell relentlessly every afternoon and all evening. Fat crimson speckled mushrooms sprouted up all around, awoken by the sudden rainfall. The rain was some relief, but the drought was soon replaced by new challenges for Jon. For instance, the simple act of using the washing machine presented a new challenge during the increasingly wet weather.

The washing machine sits on my tow cable outside, albeit under a small sheltered overhang, but the electric socket remains inside, meaning that my door has to remain open while Jon does his laundry. During the warm calm days of summer, this was never any trouble, but when it's lashing down with rain that's vertical, horizontal and everything in between, I'm in fear of a flooding.

Rummaging through various shelves and cupboards, Jon discovered a ball of string and cut off a length. Tying one end around my door handle, he fastened the door shut, preventing it from violently swinging open, smashing against my flimsy wall and blowing freezing air and rain inside. Unwittingly he had stumbled across the No.8 wire, a legacy from the old pioneering days. You can think of this wire as a metaphor for Kiwi resourcefulness, and a symbol of the improvising ingenuity of those New Zealanders who lived in the remote wop-wops. Back in the day, the No. 8 was the preferred choice of wire for creating fences around New Zealand's farms during the country's period of settlement. What was wrong with the No.7 and No.9 wire, I cannot say. But the No.8 wire proved to be so useful that it became handy for everything from replacing the handle of a bucket, to tying a caravan's door shut on a windy evening.

Take the humble bucket. In June 1928, the Ellesmere Guardian had provided a valuable guide for Canterbury readers on how to turn an old kerosene tin into a useful bucket: "Take a piece of No. 8 gauge fencing wire, about six feet long, and measuring the centre, proceed to wind it around a piece of three-quarter-inch pipe, or a broom handle..." After a couple of fiddly steps involving right-angle bends and hooking the wire to the top of the tin, hey presto: a bucket whose "handle will be found a boon, as it is somewhat elastic and gives a good grip, and is far preferable to the single wire, which cuts into the fingers". This simple bit of wire can tell you a great deal about what it means to be a Kiwi. The legacy of the No. 8 wire and New Zealand's inventive spirit was one of necessity. In a land so far from anywhere else, if you could not import it then you had to build it yourself. Fix it or do without.

The Europeans often get the credit for being so enterprising, but the Maori were highly resourceful and developed skills that astonished the Europeans. In 1819, the English army officer Richard Cruise described how a Bay of Islands chief named Tetoro had ingeniously made a stock (wooden butt) for his musket: "The place for the barrel had been hollowed out by fire, and the excavation for the lock, though made with an old knife and wretched chisel, was singularly accurate."

Now I come to think of it, as a wild caravan, I am a product of this same phenomenon. I might easily have been discarded for scrap, crushed down and deposited into landfill. Instead, someone had the bright idea to give me a new lease of life, and with this second chance they transformed the sum of my parts into this wildly eccentric home in the forest. As the Wombles would say, making good use of those things that ordinary folk leave behind.

In 1900, New Zealand had the highest number of patent applications per capita in the world. Even today, New Zealand is ranked fourth in the world for patents filed in proportion to gross domestic product (GDP), and fifth on the basis of population. The spirit of the No. 8 wire inspired some extraordinary and inventive individuals in New Zealand. There was Richard Pearse of Waitohi who built a dangerous contraption that may just have flown a few months before the Wright Brothers managed it in North Carolina. One of my favourite anecdotes is the first electric street lighting in one Nelson suburb that was powered by a small hydroelectric generator, in the hills above the city. To switch the lights on and off, a chicken run was added to the power plant. At dusk every night the chooks would go inside their coop and roost on a special hinged perch. The perch sank under their weight, and connected a switch which turned on the street lights. At first light the hens would leave the coop, the spring-loaded perch swung back and the lights went out again. I'm sure there's a joke to be made here about how many chickens does it to take to change a light bulb, but I don't do chicken jokes.

Today, you can still find people inventing some new gizmo, often in the shed at the bottom of their garden. Personally, I find sheds to be terrible bores, but I guess that's what happens if you never leave your own back garden. Horrible wooden boxes that are always losing the screwdriver you need. Yet, there's a great tradition of Kiwi men tinkering in their shed, salvaging and repairing old clocks, ham radios and Tesla generators, often inventing some contraption or another. I knew a Brian once whose shed was as big as a hangar. It was a factory really, where he restored old steam trains. He was always happiest building a new plate-steel firebox. His poor wife wanted to go on holiday but Brian couldn't bare to leave his shed. "I get withdrawal symptoms if I'm away... working with steel, and the riveting, it just gets hold of you."

One of the most memorable shed inventors was Burt Munro, who was immortalised in a movie by Anthony Hopkins. In his Invercargill home workshop, Burt converted a 1920 Indian motorcycle into the machine that set world speed records in the 1960s at the Bonneville Salt Flats in Utah. He made many of the parts and tools himself, in none other than in the shed at the bottom of his garden.

The inventive trait of the No.8 wire is often used in New Zealand's tourism industry and today, you're more likely to find someone inventing a bizarre but ingenious way of parting a thrill seeking tourist from their money. Take for instance the humble jet boat. Back in 1953, a chap named CWF Hamilton saw the need for a type of water transport that could travel through the shallow waters of New Zealand's rivers. Unlike other boats, this one doesn't have a submerged rudder and hull and instead it has a flat bottom. The boat is powered with a high octane propeller that sucks water like a hoover through the front of the boat, and spits it out of the rear. Now a tourist plaything, the jet boat was once invented out of necessity. In the absence of roads, rivers provided the only access to the more remote parts of New Zealand. Countries as far afield as Nepal, Papau New Guinea and the Amazon continue to be explored and opened up, thanks to this Kiwi invention.

Not far from me, tucked behind an innocuous petrol station is something called the Fly-by-wire. Quite possibly the ultimate evolution of the modest no.8 wire, this device is quite literally a tangle of wires and cables that hold taut a jet engine. A poor hapless individual is strapped in, before being rocketed through the air. Only in New Zealand would such a thing be found in such an out the way place. In America or Britain, this would be sat in a theme park with advertising and posters, and people selling hotdogs. Only in New Zealand, with its practical no-nonsense approach and ability to turn over any old patch of wop-wops into something enterprising, could you find a dangerous dangling rocket in such an inconspicuous place. Jon swallowed his fear of heights and went on to experience this extreme end of the No.8 wire first hand.

Thursday 24 April

What on earth was I doing, I thought as my chest was strapped to the rocket. I was past the point of no return now. I looked ahead to see a steering wheel and a throttle, but no brakes. "I'll winch you up the hill, and when I give the signal, just hit the throttle and release the safety catch" the teenage adrenalin enthusiast nonchalantly explained. I nodded nervously. "Don't worry mate," he assured me. "She'll be sweet as!"

A long cable hauled me backwards up the hillside, completely disorientating me. Hanging upside down by my feet, sixty foot from the ground, the blood drained through my body and collected in my head. A little giddy with adrenalin, my arms ached from supporting my body weight, instinctively not trusting the straps that were the only thing preventing me from falling headfirst in to the distant ground below, in a broken crumpled heap.

Oh well, here goes nothing. I tickled the throttle and hit the release catch, accelerating headfirst towards the ground. The combined force of gravity and the engine conspired to create an acceleration that well exceeded sixty miles per hour. Whistling through the air, I plunged rapidly towards the ground, gasping for breath.

A few metres from a terrible accident, the cable gracefully swung upwards in a giant arc, pulling me up the opposite side of the valley. The air rushed past and the landscape swept beneath me. I pulled the steering wheel hard left and swung around, to soar back down the valley. A herd of slightly out-of-focus sheep munched contentedly on the grass as I flew low over their heads. They were neither distracted nor impressed by yet another lunatic in a rocket. As far as the sheep were concerned, it's just another patch of grass laden wop-wops.

As my initial terror subsided I was surprised to find myself rather relaxed. Flying around, in perfect control of my motion, I admire the view and actually began to enjoy the sensation of flight. While the first few seconds of blood-pumping adrenalin had felt like an eternity, the seven minutes of flight passed in a moment, and all too soon, I'm quickly returned to the safety of both my feet being firmly on the ground. "I told yer she'd be sweet." he said reassuringly, before pausing for a moment. "But we did have one accident, the poor lady just crashed into the take-off point, terrible that was…"

End of diary entry

A caravan is not a large space in which to live, and there are times when Jon gets restless. Today, he's shut my door and set out to climb Mt Mananui which is the forested peak that's directly opposite us. He doesn't have a map and no one knows where he's gone. Hopeless! I may be fussing like a mother protecting its young, but if he trips and falls in the bush, then that bottle of water and couple of bananas won't last long.

Despite being autumn, it felt like a summer's day, with the sun cheerfully burning its UV waves through the hole in the ozone layer. The distant roar of quad bikes compete with the rustling of the surrounding branches in the gentle breeze. The local bird life twitter and squawk, warning one another that there is a strange visitor in their midst.

I watch as he disappears from view, having crossed the Maungakotukutuku Road and clambered past a colossal rimu tree, almost twice as tall as any other tree in the entire forest. The rimu is an impressive example of the indigenous tree, once prolific across New Zealand. Unfortunately, like the giant kauri trees, their hard wood makes a very fine set of furniture.

A couple hours pass before Jon stumbles out of the forest, tired, muddy and slightly confused if I'm any judge. "No trail, no path, just these red plastic tags every hundred feet or so. I thought I was lost!" Yes, he's talking to himself - again. I do wonder if he's losing it. He's lived in the bush for several weeks now and for long periods without any company. He will learn that sooner or later, something comes along to fill the silence.

Chapter 4

The transcendental caravan

T his place. It changes you. I've been out here, isolated in the bush for some years now and I can tell you, living in a remote place without any company for any length of time will change your state of mind. And if it can affect a caravan, you can be sure it's sent a few new synaptic pulses coursing through Jon's head too.

Tuesday 6 May

I put my book down, pulled not one, but two jumpers on and ventured outside to take a look at the cloudless night sky. Brrr! True, it was cold, freezing probably but the view was breathtaking. The moon was out, or at least some of it was, and the Milky-Way stretched across the sky like a colossal halo embracing the planet. The Southern Cross stood proud, forever pointing north. I turned around to look at my caravan, its windows filled with light, surrounded by the stars and darkness, reminding me of a satellite. Lost and far away, suspended in space, I imagined an astronomer might observe me from afar.

I stood there a while, quietly watching and taking in the view. I tasted the chilled air, with a sense of time winding down a gear. Then there was a palpable jolt, like a quiet earthquake that left no physical impression. There was no crack in the earth, but there had been a change nonetheless – a profound and intoxicating sensation.

For a moment, I was disconnected. I felt strangely without form, somehow insubstantial and insignificant. Lost, like a speck on a rock in the darkness. At least it might have been a moment, it may well have been much longer. Moments may have been minutes, minutes might have been hours. Time ceased to have any meaning.

I'd stumbled across something that is not easy to express. It was the feeling of utter isolation, of removal not just from society, but from the world and then finally being removed from my own sense of self. And yet, something intangible was filling this void and it pushed a tickle up my spine.

The sense of isolation quickly dissipated and instead of feeling lost, I had the profound experience of being a part of everything – the earth, air and stars - all of it. I was utterly overwhelmed by this new awareness. Although I hadn't moved a muscle, I could feel my mind recoil and flap about wildly in an effort to grasp something familiar. My subconscious struggled desperately to find a cultural reference point to cling to. David Bowman swam past, cast adrift in the final moments of 2001: A Space Odyssey, calling out to Bowie's Major Tom.

And then, as quickly as it happened, the moment passed. I was returned to reality with something like an elastic twang. I'd not so much been thrown but catapulted back to this

small patch of damp grass on a cold night,
having been in an unexplainable place. What
on earth was that? One thing I was sure of, I
was desperate for a steaming hot mug of tea.

End of diary entry

I can't say that I was entirely surprised by this turn of events. Don't get me wrong. It isn't that Jon fills his time on his knees praying or omming to himself in tranquil meditation. He hasn't done any of these things. He did attempt a few yoga moves once, but quickly abandoned the idea after almost punching nose first through my ceiling. He gave me quite a ding.

You see, time slows down in the wop-wops. I have a clock but Jon had long since turned it around to face the wall. This simple act meant that time was no longer chopped into a torrent of passing seconds and minutes, but instead ebbs almost glacially by. Only the birds and clouds passing overhead mark the passing of the present, into the future.

And it's not just the absence of a clock. As a caravan dragged from one end of this country to the other, down quiet country lanes through to the bumper-to-bumper congestion that is Auckland, I've made an observation. When you're surrounded by cars and people in a rush, it quickens the pace. You need to hurry along, keep up or you'll be left behind. Conversely, here in the bush, there is no such traffic, no people and no particular hurry. Life is slower in quiet places simply because there are fewer things to measure the passage of time against. The rapid stop watch of a city is replaced with the slower pace of a sun dial - one that fills your entire surroundings. When Jon arrived here he'd rush to and fro, frantic and quickly, but now he's slowed down. He sits and watches, relaxing and observing his surroundings. I've seen him sit for an hour or so, just watching the sunlight and shadows gradually ebb and flow from this forested landscape.

In the city you need to block your senses to prevent yourself from being overwhelmed. Trust me, in the past I'd often tune out the honking of inpatient horns, the jostling crowds and traffic became an indistinct blur as I passed by, or more often, they passed me by. The wilderness provides the opportunity to retune and hear those few and small sounds, to listen to them and pay attention. Little by little, Jon is tuning his ear into the sounds of the forest. He becomes less agitated, and pauses to listen to the sounds of wildlife that have replaced the sonic of the city. The almost constant buzz and click of insects as they go about their business, the distant call of an owl, the cry of a possum and the leaves shaking in the breeze.

Some time ago, a copy of the American classic Walden came my way. The book is an account of the writer Thoreau's life of relative solitude in the woods in Massachusetts in 1845. He lived in a wood cabin, a rather more sturdy home than what my walls can offer. Much had changed in the intervening century and a half, but it amused me when he commented with disdain about time wasted thanks to the distractions of the penny post and the magnetic telegraph. What would he have made of the constant bombardment of information that immerses everyone today? Nowadays people surround themselves with so many things, so many distractions, that I wonder if they are trying to escape from themselves.

Wednesday 21 May

I stood on my personal hilltop, helplessly in awe of my home and location. The flimsy walls that separate me from the wild landscape might have been a source of fear, but they were not. At least, not during the warm glow of the autumn nights when the natural heat of the sun warmed the caravan. It was a simple joy and a true privilege to live so close to the forest, and so far from the typical trappings of human habitation. I could look out over the mountains beyond and imagine all the things I should see - housing estates, high-rise buildings, busy roads, traffic and people, noise and pollution. There was none of that. Just a simple scene of evergreen forested mountains, the hues of light shifting and changing, transforming this ever changing but always beautiful landscape. At night, I'd switch off the lights and watch the stars pop out one by one, as if they'd arranged it carefully among themselves. After a while, I did not need to go outside because the warm, inviting outdoors came inside to me.

By living in the caravan, I'd discarded those solid walls that separate most people from their natural environment. The seasons can easily pass without being noticed, when your home has double glazing and central heating. When you live in a comfortable bubble surrounded by familiar furniture and furnishings, the outside world is safely locked out. But in the van, the barriers between my home and the natural environment were transient. The walls were a thin cavity of aluminium and plywood, and unlike a brick and mortar house the structure is insubstantial, and the windows panoramic. This is a strangely ethereal existence, neither fully exposed to the outdoors, nor does it provide the warm cosy comfort of being indoors. There are no curtains, but as the sun gently slides behind the eastern mountains each night, the gradual darkness seemed like the blinds were being drawn.

There was little to separate my simple domestic life from the wonderfully picturesque outdoors, and this vast beguiling world was leaking into my inner world. Living with a view such as this, night after night, I cannot help but acknowledge the immensity of the wilderness. But I was troubled. I'm an atheist, or at least an unenthusiastic agnostic. How was I supposed to explain such a soul expanding experience? Was this really a well aimed bolt of lightning from the Almighty?

Turning over the conflict again and again, I entertain the idea of turning prophet. I imagined going to strangers in the street with the simple revelation that living in a remote place can transform your life, perhaps even place you closer to God. I'd shout from the hilltops "Leave your home and move to the forest!" and extoll the virtues of living in a hut in the hills. I wonder how I'd try to put into words the seismic effect that living in the woods can have - that fundamental ripple through your very core. Maybe I'd start my own religion. Caravanism? Caravanity? Caravanology?

End of diary entry

Has Jon totally lost the plot? Maybe, maybe not. I must say, a faith based on caravans is a flattering if unlikely prospect, but he isn't the first person to be affected by the quiet power of wild places.

In my limited experience, Maori have a particularly acute awareness of New Zealand's nature. "The forest and earth is your family, eh," I remember this old lady telling her kids, in a desperate effort to stop them pulling branches off a tree. Like many Maori, she could trace her descent all the way back to the original Polynesian settlers, some eight hundred years ago. Genealogy might be a casual hobby for some people, but for the Maori this is a core part of their sense of identity. It's referred to as whakapapa, which might sound like a village fete game where you replaced the mole shaped sock with an ageing Frenchman, but it is a very serious business. At least, it still is for some. I remember her young hoons were less interested.

Nevertheless, she and many others believe that their first ancestors were the heavens and earth - the parents of all living things, including the sea, the forest, the birds and the people. There is at least some truth to it. I have seen one of these mythical beings for myself. If you care to look, there are living gods hiding away deep in the forest. I once paid a visit to Tane Mahuta. The Maori god of the forest is the largest of the vertiginous kauri trees - a giant amid a forest of giants. This tree, a lively sapling during the time of Christ, is more than two thousand years old. Tane is believed to stand so tall that it holds the sky aloft, bringing light into the world. As he towered over my meagre ten feet, from tyre to roof, I had vertigo just looking at him.

Traditionally, the Maori cannot fell a tree without first performing a certain tikanga or custom. There's the old story of Rātā, who cut down a tree to carve it into a canoe. When he returned the next day to continue his task, the tree was miraculously standing back in its original position. He felled it again and set to work, but the same thing happened the next day, and the next. Finally, Rātā hid behind a bush and saw the hakuturi (forest guardians in the form of birds, insects and other life) replanting the tree. When he confronted them, they explained that he had failed to perform the correct rites. He then performed the ritual, and the hakuturi released the tree.

The belief in forest spirits may have influenced the Maori relations with the first Europeans. Pakehakeha are pale spirit beings believed to live deep in the forests and mountaintops in New Zealand. I must say, I've never spotted one in all my travels. Secretive creatures, their presence is revealed by ethereal flute music and singing. Not to be confused with folk musicians, the spirits are said to be hostile and protective of their land, not unlike the European settlers. It's not much of a leap of imagination to link the Pakehakeha to the word Pakeha, which refers to the Europeans.

Maori culture and religion may be strongly interlinked with the wilderness, but the connection of nature and spirituality is not unique to New Zealand. I was rather fond of an old yogee who stayed with me for some time. Wiry fella, lean as a bean thanks to a diet of lentil dhal. Years ago, we'd roll up to some excluded spot where he'd practice his graceful movements outside, whatever the weather, come rain or shine, summer or winter.

Visitors would swing by sometimes, but not often. For a while I thought he was just a bit of a loner, I liked him though, he always looked after me, carefully wiping the veggie curry from my formica. He enjoyed company when it came by and was a hospitable soul, ready to share whatever he had which wasn't much, it must be said. On one such occasion, a visitor asked why he chose to spend so much time alone in this van. His answer took me by surprise; he said that the worst thing you can meet in the jungle isn't a snake or some other predator, but rather another person.

He found that animals were predicable creatures in any given situation, while humans often don't say what they're thinking, and are much harder to trust. I'd vouch for that. At least with a possum I know it wants to either scratch, mutilate or defecate on me. People? You never can tell. He explained that it's much more difficult to reach nirvana when you are distracted, especially when trying to second guess peoples' behaviour and motives. His idea of nirvana was not a perfect state of ecstasy, but actually a sense of calm, that's free from reaction, jealousy or anger. So, he chose a simple life, largely removed from civilisation and the rest of the world. Weeks would go by in virtual silence before another visitor came by, to ask questions.

Another visitor explained that his life was in turmoil, he was exhausted and his time was in constant demand. "Why is it so difficult to hang on to a single thought before it is blown away by a thousand others?" he asked. The wise old yogee swept his hand through the air, indicating that he knew it wasn't easy, indicating his reasons for leaving everything behind to stay here, with me. "Don't take my word for it," he explained. "Scientists say that everything began with a simple energy that caused the Big Bang. Gradually that simple energy formed complex particles that became matter. These small building blocks gathered together to create stars and planets, such as ours. You see, in the beginning everything was simple and ever since, all matter and life has become more complicated. People may have self awareness now, but we have evolved and were once primates. Life is increasingly complex, and that is why yours is overwhelming."

The yogee was a lapsed Catholic, and found his purpose in the wilderness having fled the strict doctrines of the church. It's a shame he never met another resident of mine, he'd have been surprised by how much they had in common. She was a nun and her name was Sister Wendy. She would take me away for a holiday, and sit quietly and pray. I don't know why she wasn't in a convent, I just assumed she'd escaped for a change in scenery. She'd not say much, but when she did, people listened: "One of the things prayer will do is show you yourself, and that is something most of us will go to a lot of trouble to avoid" she'd say. Despite their obvious differences, the nun and the yogee both had strong beliefs, and shared an understanding of the power of silence, nature and a good caravan.

I've had Bibles on my bookshelf, volumes of Sufi poetry and a Koran or two. As vans go I'm pretty well read, and I have sussed a few things out. Strip away the centuries of dogma and ritual, and an awful lot of religions have at their core a sense of silence and solitude. A silent mind, freed from distraction is an important step to spiritual development. Don't take my word for it, look at the wilderness prophets of Biblical times. Jesus is said to have spent 40 days and nights alone in the desert. John the Baptist is described as someone "in the wilderness". Elijah travelled for forty days and forty nights to a cave to hear the "still small voice" of God.

The young Muhammad had the habit of meditating alone for several weeks every year in a cave on Mt. Hira. In Islam it's highly recommended to go on a self-retreat, to isolate yourself and attempt to fully understand who you are, what you want, and what you are going to do about it all.

Yonks before his enlightenment the Buddha too spent extended periods alone in the forest. Reminiscing on this time many years later, he said: "Such was my seclusion that I would plunge into some forest and live there. If I saw a cowherd, shepherd, grass-cutter, wood-gatherer or forester, I would flee so that they would not see me or me them."

You people, you fill your modern lives with distractions. A constant barrage of information at your fingertips, some of which can be enriching, and much of which but can be engulfing. Finding the space and time to pause for long enough to explore your own mind is not easy. But living an unhurried life allows your thoughts to percolate, and enables you to focus on the most vital and significant experiences. The point I'm trying to make is that you're probably more likely to have a religious or spiritual experience, call it what you will, in a caravan in the woods than in a traditional church or temple.

Tuesday 27 May

The rational part of my mind kicked in, and I quickly realised that caravanology would be met with derision and laughter. And I'd understand such a reaction, because that's precisely how I would have responded if someone had told me this tale.

My inner atheist has won the struggle, having sat me down and patiently explained to me that while something strange had indeed occurred, there was no evidence to suggest the intervention of an all powerful deity. I hadn't witnessed God, but there was no doubt that I had a highly unusual and profound experience and one that was totally new to me.

I can only refer to what I noticed, felt and sensed at the time, which is a brief period of calmness, like the eye of a hurricane where I had no concept of past, present and future. The whole thing is equally liberating and to be honest quite terrifying, because it's the mental equivalent of falling off of a cliff. Losing sense of the usual reality that I was accustomed to, my reaction was to reach out and haul myself back to normality. With hindsight I'd like to have remained there a little longer, but I suspect it takes time and patience and a receptive mind to not recoil in alarm. Once glimpsed, it's one of those moments I might spend the rest of my life searching for...

End of diary entry

I'm relieved that as a caravan, I'm spared this obsession with God. I know who my creators were. There was an assembly line of men in an industrial estate near Auckland. Sheets of metal and parts went in and caravans came out – a simple enough process. But people, you do like to complicate matters.

Admittedly, I did question my existence when I was first brought to the wop-wops. I wasn't just brought here as I was in effect, exiled. They removed my wheels and replaced them with tree stumps. Can you imagine? All my life I'd travelled the roads, exploring here, there and everywhere. Then I was left in the bush, with no means to escape. It took quite some time to adapt to being surrounded by trees and the vast sky of glittering stars above. If I am no longer what I was - a means of transport, then what am I? Thankfully, I know I am not just a van alone, but a lone caravan and Kiwi icon.

Chapter 5

On the road

I t's been some years since my tires touched tarmac. Hell, it's been a while since I had wheels on at all, but in the days before I was a lone caravan, I was on the road and my, what roads they are. Indulge my reminisces for a moment. I used to love a long journey on the open road, the wind whistling through my windows and the scenery changing from one moment to the next. One particular favourite route was State Highway 8, passing Lake Tekapo, a great sweeping vista of black tarmac weaving through uninterrupted plateaus of tree lined valleys, dipping through azure lakes.

If you don't mind the rain, the SH6 is a great road, skirting the rugged and wind-swept West Coast of the South Island. You pass some of the greatest scenery in all of New Zealand. If coastal drives are your thing, then you definitely won't be disappointed after driving from Westport to Greymouth. The mighty Tasman Sea pounds the coast on your right while the snow-capped Southern Alps stand majestically on your left, with the drizzle of sea spray on your windows...

Some of the finest driving can be found on the road to Milford Sounds, in the largely uninhabited Fjiordland. I vividly remember a blanket of mist enveloping the surrounding mountains and the grazing deer. Glimpses of Fjordland's beech forest tease their way through the morning haze, until the landscape gradually reveals itself. Steep mountain peaks appear, unveiled by thick waves of foggy cloud that rub out scenery like a giant eraser. The view, when finally revealed, was all the more remarkable for its gradual unveiling.

This road is not without its drama though. The same route to Milford Sounds includes the roughly hewn Homer Tunnel, a 1,200 metre long passage of terror, carved into a granite mountain. Made me nervous every time I passed through there. Way back when, work had begun on the tunnel during the Great Depression. In freezing conditions, men with calloused hands smashed through the impenetrable granite using hammers and dynamite. These were tough men in difficult times, a long way from home, and many of them died in the effort. One man would hold a sharp metal rod against the rock face (presumably having picked the short straw) whilst another wielded a sledge hammer. Once they'd created a crack in the rock, a stick of dynamite was wedged into the crevice, and gradually (they started in 1935, and completed the tunnel in 1953) more than a kilometre of granite was blown out of the mountain.

I remember driving through the confines of the tunnel, as rough jagged rocks peeked through the darkness. Water dripped constantly from the roof, and there wasn't a single light or pair of cat's eyes along its entire length. One careless slip of the steering wheel and car, man and caravan might easily be sliced in half along these sharp granite walls. I'd speed down the narrow lane, with only an occasional metal bracket overhead supporting the tonnes of mountain above me. I'd then emerge into the light at the end of the tunnel with immense relief, incredulous that there were cyclists brave enough to venture through. Some fifty years later, the tunnel has never been modernised or concreted over, and remains as treacherous as the day it was built.

New Zealanders love their roads and are addicted to cars, and it's easy to see why. Trust me, there's nothing like an open stretch of cool tarmac, leading all the way to the horizon to give you a sense of purpose and wonder. I hear there are more cars per person in New Zealand than anywhere else on the planet, except for Luxembourg and

Iceland. You wouldn't know it though. Aside from the suffocating gridlock and traffic jams that is Auckland, there's plenty of space for car and motor home alike. Ours is a sparsely populated country with such rugged and remote terrain that the car is the ideal transport solution. No doubt, the popularity of the car and the absence of a decent rail network contributed to the popularity of us caravans, too. That, and our glowing personality, of course.

Of course, there are far more cows than cars. Not that you can, or should, ride a cow to work. It's worth mentioning this ratio of cows to cars because as a signee of the Kyoto Treaty, New Zealand pledged to reduce its green house gas emissions. In an extraordinary twist, whilst the rest of the developed world explores ways of reducing damage caused by vehicles, in New Zealand the government's latest initiative is to tax cows. The collective clouds of methane emanating from cows backsides produce enough green-house gases to cause a serious environmental problem. Instead of politely asking the cows to stop letting off wind or putting a cork in it, the government have instead decided to fine the farmers in the form of a tax and contribute the money towards eco-friendly projects to offset the bovines emissions. 'Farmers Against Ridiculous Taxation (FART)' are in uproar. Understandably, whilst the whole idea of a fart tax is really rather funny, the farmers aren't finding any of this especially amusing. The newspapers ran a headline photo of a tractor half-way up the entrance to the Beehive, New Zealand's parliament. Crowds of angry farmers blockaded parliament in protest. The cows continue to fart a hole through the ozone layer.

Meanwhile, people continue to drive like there's no tomorrow. Make no mistake, driving is a hazardous occupation because the New Zealand driver, with a few good natured exceptions, pays no heed to the rules of the road. I've seen them overtake a funeral procession on a blind switchback bend and many a time I've been tailgated down a mountain for the sake of thirty seconds. I have a theory on this and again, it's the wop-wops effect. These terrifying driving habits might have something to do with a law that enables youngsters to begin their driving rampage at the youthful age of fifteen. You can't vote, get married, buy a house or drink alcohol, but you can drive a car. In the ye olde days, the thinking was that in remote areas, if you couldn't drive then you might not be able to leave your own property, at least not without embarking on a five-day hike.

Today, New Zealand has a thriving boy-racer culture, where youngsters spend their pocket money and ill-gotten gains on lowering suspensions, fuel injection systems and go faster stripes. I have been parked by the roadside and witnessed many illegal road races at the dead of night, with tires scorching blackened lines down the freeways. Another popular past-time is chaining your car to a post in the backyard, and driving around in circles until the tyres vaporise, or the fire brigade arrives. And, no, I've never seen anyone attempt this with a caravan. But you can't blame it all on the kids, as many adult Kiwis who are old enough to know better continue to drive like hormonal teenagers for their entire lives, potentially turning this quiet country into the world's largest racing circuit.

I've had more than my fair share of bumps, scrapes and collisions. I've been to the panel beaters more than a few times to iron the dings out. Honestly, it's a wonder my axle never snapped, but enough of my mishaps. Instead I'll tell you about Jon's recent crash; a cautionary tale of the mad men lurking on quiet country roads. Thank god for part-time police and small town hospitality.

Saturday 7 June

A loud squeal of burnt tires erupted from out of nowhere, and an oncoming car careered towards us. He'd taken the bend ahead too fast and lost control, his rear tyres spun out, leaving a trail of black skid marks burnt down the road. Wow, that was lucky, I thought. It looked, for a moment, as if the out of control driver was just going to miss us. The relief was soon punctured by a CRUNCH as the oncoming car punched us clean off the road. The other car spun 360 degrees before coming to a stop.

"Everyone ok?" I asked. I was travelling with friends who were visiting from London. David, Andrea and I were a little shaken but there didn't seem to be any broken limbs or pools of blood. I opened the passenger side door and went to check on the other driver. "You alright there, mate?" I said to a man in his early forties with close cropped hair. He jumped from his car, walked around the pieces of scattered wreckage, and swaggered up to me, a little too close for comfort. I could smell his breath and it wasn't pretty.

"What the hell d'ye think you were doing on my side of the road?" he ranted furiously, looking agitated, shifting from one foot to the other. I was taken aback. "What do you mean?" I asked. "You just lost control of your car, came around that bend too fast and smashed us off the road. Look, you can see the tyre marks." I pointed at the road. "Your car is on our side of the road..."

"Don't you blaady tell me it was my fault," he retaliated. "You're just a blaady liar. That was the worst driving I've ever seen!" I tried to calm him down. He was drunk or worse, which was useful if the police ever arrived, but he was also very aggressive and more than slightly unhinged. I tried to placate him, just in case he kept a sharpened hatchet in the boot of his car. Meanwhile, Andrea, who'd been driving, had realised that he was trying to blame her for the accident. She gave him a stinging rebuke, and I thought for one awful moment he would smack her one. I interrupted the shouting match, suggesting we swapped insurance details.

He paced about his car, his behaviour increasingly erratic and nervous. "Name's Liam Dearsley," he answered, as he pulled tufts of grass out of the ground, using them to wipe the dented remains of his front bumper. It was a start. "So what's your telephone number?" I asked. "Erm, its 4789 mumble mumble," his voice trailing off. "Sorry I didn't quite get that... Could you repeat it please?" Again, he said "4978 mumble mumble". This was hopeless. "Sorry, I'm still not quite getting it. Say it again?"

Meanwhile, Andrea had walked to a nearby garage for assistance. We were fortunate there was help to hand because apart from the garage, we hadn't seen any sign of life for many miles. Dearsley, having realised the game was up, had returned to his car, started up the engine and fled the scene. We on the other hand, weren't going anywhere. I turned the ignition key and put the car into first. The engine turned once, lurched forward a couple of feet and promptly died on the grass verge. The front axle had snapped.

It wasn't looking good. We hadn't got his insurance details, our car was a write-off and there was an excess of $1,300 on the car rental insurance. Most worrying of all, there was a strong likelihood that this lunatic didn't have any insurance at all.

In New Zealand there's no legal requirement for car insurance. I didn't exactly welcome the prospect of being a thousand bucks out of pocket, but for the moment I was more concerned with being broken down in the middle of nowhere, with no transport. Fortunately, we had a stroke of luck. The elderly couple who ran the garage had ushered us into their kitchen and offered us a pot of tea, along with plenty of sympathy. "Oh we heard the scream of his brakes, don't you worry it wasn't your fault love. Here, have a biscuit."

I sipped the sweet tea, made the necessary phone calls and it wasn't so long before the law arrived. Stepping through the glass patio doors, the policeman was so enormous, that for a moment he eclipsed the sun and cast the room into shadow. He was casually dressed in a t-shirt and pair of shorts, which seemed a bit informal, even in these parts. "You caught me cleaning out the pool when you rang," he explained, as if this was normal behaviour for an officer of the law. We provided our statements as the policeman scratched some notes.

Speaking into his walkie-talkie he ordered four squad cars to apprehend the fugitive driver. Four cars? I could hardly believe it. In most other places, you'd be lucky to get that kind of response if you'd been murdered. "Well, it's been a quiet day," he explained, and it seemed unlikely that the police encountered many pandemic crime waves out here in the wop-wops. "So could you give me your name, address and details then?" he asked me. This was something of a problem.

I desperately tried to think of my address
but I just didn't have one. I attempted to
explain, but failed hopelessly. "I'm living
here, in a caravan, in the Maungakotukutukus,
in the bush...I don't have an address because
the postman won't deliver to us, because
we're too far from town." The policeman
towered over me and frowned. He looked at
me suspiciously, as if he'd never heard so
much nonsense in all his life. "I think I can
remember my postal box though," I faltered.
"Um, will that do?"

Squeezing into the back of the police
Land Rover with our luggage, we were kindly
offered a lift to Christchurch. Chatting
away, he revealed that as well as cleaning
his swimming pool and being a policeman,
he farmed alpacas in his spare time. The
radio crackled into life. A squad car had
apprehended Dearsley down a side street,
while he was trying to give the police the
slip. Intriguingly the crackling voice added
that Dearsley was a "patient". The officer
wouldn't elaborate on what sort of patient,
but we figured that we'd been smashed off the
road by an escapee from a mental hospital.

We were taken to the local police station
in Darfield where the policeman went to
find his trousers, before paying a visit
to headquarters in Christchurch. We were
briefly left in charge of the station until
he returned. "Help yourselves to coffee,"
he said hospitably. "But don't answer the
telephone, and don't let anyone in until I
come back."

Left in charge of a provincial police
station, we made the most of the situation,

helping ourselves to a cuppa, and using the phone to book a hostel for the night. I'd heard that people in the smaller communities of New Zealand were trusting types, but this was staggering. The computer had been left switched on and the police station's email account was on display. We were so impressed by the hospitality and efficiency of the local Kiwi policeman and llama farmer that we returned the favour by leaving our mugs clean and dry, and resisted the temptation to load his rifle and try some target practice.

End of diary entry

I can't say that I miss the hazards of the road, but besides admiring the towering mountains, vertiginous volcanoes and phosphorescent grassy meadows, I used to amuse myself by spotting the peculiar letterboxes by the roadside. Creating your own hand-crafted scale replica of your home is a Kiwi tradition, and these mini homes are stood outside the drive to be used as a letterbox. Like a dolls house, every detail is replicated in miniature, with tiny tiles painted on the roof, and little windows and doors, and sometimes even their own miniature letter box that's the size of a matchstick. I guess it was the No. 8 wire phenomenon at work again, where people made what they needed instead of buying a mass produced product.

I used to pass my time on the road by spotting these quirky letterboxes scattered across both the North and South Islands. They come in all sorts of unusual varieties. Some resemble grinning friesian cows, another looked like a round-faced pig. One letterbox had been bizarrely made out of an old lawnmower and one farm had set an entire fridge outside their gate, presumably in case the mail got too warm. I never did spot a miniature caravan letterbox though. They do make for an interesting distraction - you'd be shocked and dismayed at how often my tyres sighed at the sight of another endless sublime soaring mountain and rolling hill.

Ok. I had a letterbox obsession, but it was harmless. I'm fond of people too, sometimes. I particularly liked the fleeting company of hitch hikers. As a nomad myself, I have some empathy for these hapless creatures waiting on the kerb, always on the move from one place to another. You'd have thought there were enough cars to go around in this country, since there's twice as many cars as people, but there is a strong tradition of hitch hiking in New Zealand. I hear hitch hiking has all but vanished in Britain and disappeared along with hippies and free love in the USA. New Zealand may be one of the few English speaking countries that still has hitch hikers. Why? I cannot say, although if you're waiting for a bus to take you to the next town, you may die of old age and disappointment. I cannot count the number of times a stranger has stood by the roadside, arm out stretched, thumbing for a lift. Most often we just passed them by, their stories untold, but sometimes we picked them up to help out and listen to their tales.

There was one hitch-hiker, I don't recall her name, a San Franciscan in her autumn years with wild white hair, and a spark in her voice that suggested she hadn't lost any of her energy since Woodstock. She was smoking some pungent Afghan weed that made my windows all hazy. I hiccuped so hard I burst a tyre. "My mother always wanted to live in New Zealand, and we stayed here for a number of years while I cared for her before she died. Now I'm back here visiting friends and well, I'd like to stay, but..." She paused. "I was staying at a hostel up in the Northland. Y'know way out in the middle of nowhere, real boondocks. I'd been chatting to the hostel manager, and told him about my situation, how I wanted to stay in the country, but couldn't, not without marrying a New Zealander. I'd only been joking, but he was very understanding and said that he could arrange something. He had this gentleman friend in Auckland called Granny, who might be able to make some kind of arrangement."

The hostel manager had then attempted to arrange a marriage of convenience between the San Franciscan and Granny, who I imagined to be some camp sort of Noel Coward fellow. The plan was that a little cash would change hands and they would be married in name only, living separate lives, before amicably divorcing. "Except, Granny changed his mind, and instead I arranged a pre-nuptial agreement with the hostel owner. We agreed that I would help him run the hostel for a year or two, we'd have separate rooms and we'd divorce after three or four years. But things didn't quite work out, let's just say that his intentions weren't exactly honourable. He was twenty years younger than me, and I never thought sex would come into it. Anyway after we married, and I was living at the hostel and helping to run the place, I discovered that he was filming guests with hidden cameras in all the double rooms, and selling pornographic videos..."

Another hitch hiker was young Chrissie, an infectious force of nature who exuded warmth and confidence. She had big blonde curls and despite the possible dangers of hitch-hiking from one end of New Zealand to the other, she had met a series of extraordinary people who had returned her good nature and offered nothing but generous hospitality.

"One time," said Chrissie, bubbling with enthusiasm, "this super friendly guy pulls over, and gives us a lift to Lake Taupo. He was a salesman for Tui beer. Anyway, after two hours driving, my friend Karin freaks out! She'd left her camera back at the hostel. I tried to calm her, telling her we'll ring the hostel and get it sent to us, but Tui man, he won't have it. He turns the car around and drives us two hours out of his way to collect the camera. So we're sitting there, telling one another stories and we stop to look at a ravine. He laughed and said that it would nice to take his jet boat out on the river. A couple of hours later, we're jetboating with his two daughters, having the time of our lives - although my legs were hurting for the next week! His family let us stay over for the night. And when we left, he gave us Tui shirts, Tui hats, Tui scarves, Tui socks and Tui sunglasses. It was a perfect moment."

She'd found no shortage of offers of a lift, although not everyone had been so fortunate. Recounting another story, she showed the flip-side to honest rural New Zealand life. "I'd just arrived at the hostel and was making a cup of tea, when this flustered looking Canadian kinda stumbled into the kitchen," Chrissie explained. "He was a proper Canadian though, not one of those Americans pretending by plastering their bags with maple leaves. He had this serious, sort of haunted look about him. Told me he'd just escaped after hitching to the hostel. He'd parted from his friends out in the wop-wops, and tried to flag down a car."

"Quite a few passed him by and he was beginning to wonder if one would ever stop, when this beat up old truck pulled over, just sort of dissolving from rust. And then this scruffy face with a beard peered out of the window. 'Boy, ye lookin for a ride?' 'Uh, yeah, sort of', he replied. 'Well, we got just enough room for you,' he offered. The Canadian, he was pretty scared, but got into the car anyway. Sitting on the backseat was this huge dog, who kept growling in the Canadian's ear, stinking of bad breath. The driver sparked up this huge joint, took a deep puff, and offered it to the Canadian, who was too terrified to turn him down."

"There was nothing on the road for miles, they were in the middle of nowhere, and the driver was telling him about all the people who'd been killed on the road. 'A girl in 1989, buried right here, a car, there, which had rolled over onto someone'. The Canadian was already freaked out, when the driver suddenly turned the truck around. 'Boy, d'ya smell 'em?' he said, talking to his dog. 'Dya smell possum, boy?' The dog was barking in a frenzy and they pulled over. The driver got out of the truck with a shotgun in his hand and walked towards a ditch. The Canadian just sat there, quietly praying he'll get out of this alive. Fifteen minutes later, the guy dropped him off in town and shook his hand. 'Boy, it was nice meeting you' he'd said and drove off."

Before leaving, Chrissie pulled out a photo of another couple who had offered her a lift. The elderly pair might easily have lived on the frontier two hundred years ago, the woman adorned in a bonnet and old fashioned colonial dress, him with a check shirt and long tufty hair, holding a garden rake in his hand. Kind souls, although from the photo you might mistake them for ghosts.

They reminded me of the tale of a father and his young son who'd broken down one dark, windswept night along the Desert Road. Hailing a lift from a passing vehicle, they'd thanked the driver for rescuing them from their plight. The driver leered at the pair, disturbingly regaling his passengers of past accidents along the road. "One man and his son were hitch-hiking just along this road, but they chose the wrong car. The driver brutally murdered the pair of them." The passengers on the backseat looked at one another. "I know," said the boy, "we were the ones who were killed..."

New Zealand is a country well suited for a road trip, if you can dodge the oncoming traffic and get out the way quickly enough from the guy tailgating your rear bumper. There's plenty enough space between destinations to appreciate a couple of hours drive through the scenic route. Trust me though, a scenic route is not a journey to be taken lightly. In this caravan's experience a scenic route will typically include two features. The first is that it will, of course, provide a pretty, if not dramatic view of the surrounding landscape. The second is that it will probably be a near terrifying journey of hairpin bends, landslides, and lunatic drivers. I remember along one lane a sign hung outside a local bookbinder's. With typical Kiwi bluntness, it summed up the New Zealand driving experience: "Bill's Bookbinders. Slow down you bastards! Speed kills!"

Speed isn't the only thing that can kill you, of course. I can tell you a story or two. One time, I was enthusiastically pulled along the scenic route through the Whanganui National park, despite being rather too narrow for me. An area with a long Maori tradition, the missionaries arrived in the 1840s, renaming tribal villages after Christian cities, and established churches and a convent. The distinctive angular maraes were present in Hiruharama, Ranana, Koriniti and Atene, translating as Jerusalem, London, Corinth and Athens. The nuns of the convent had long since passed on or moved away from the remote clapboard convent. Rumour persists that one very ancient nun still resides there, creaking about the wooden floorboards of the convent like a living ghost. The poignancy wasn't lost on me, particularly when the loose stones of the scrappy unsealed road pummeled me like gunfire.

We arrived in Pipiriki and the unsealed path became even more rutted and cratered, as we drove along a track cut deep into the valley face, the Whanganui River flowing forcefully below us. Something was wrong. Somehow we had left the road behind and ended up on a disused track that disappeared deep into the bush. My suspension creaked with displeasure as I was very carefully manoeuvered through a three-point turn. To be honest, it was probably closer to a fifteen-point turn, before I was turned around. Below us, by the river's edge was a scrap yard of rusting cars - past casualties perhaps. With a sigh of relief I was returned to the road, having managed to avoid falling into the river or joining the scrap-yard.

My driver that day was Joe, who had briefly stepped out for directions. He headed over to the Park Office, which seemed totally deserted. So he went to knock on the door of a nearby house. It was an ageing wooden clapboard house, white paint peeling off the veranda. Its curtains were drawn and the building had the distinctive smell of decay about it. An old pair of pants hung unpleasantly on the washing line. Walking up to the building, he was within a few steps of knocking on the door when a creeping nervousness took over and he dashed back into his car. I didn't blame him. It looked like a scene from The Amityville Horror or The Texas Chainsaw Massacre.

Joe spotted a friendly looking Maori woman standing outside a sign for the local Medical Centre. We pulled into the drive to ask the way. "Kia Ora", he called out, "can you show me the way to Raetihi?" She stopped what she was doing and eyed him warily, as her husband stepped out of the house. He had greying hair and his eyes were rolling about in their sockets. Gesturing towards the road, his arms were waving about all over the place in a twitchy, manic fashion. Without uttering a word, he indicated that we ought to continue along the road. There was some confusion, as Joe questioned his directions. The man with the rotating eyeballs stepped out of view for a moment. "He's got a gun!" "What?" The man had returned and there was a rifle case in his hands. You'd be surprised how quickly a car can move whilst towing a caravan, but we surely left there as quickly as we possibly could. Ours was a lucky escape. I'd heard numerous stories of drug abuse in rural outback areas, especially among Maori communities. He looked like he'd been liberally helping himself to the Medical Centre's supplies.

Chapter 6

We don't all live in the bush y'know

Glacially carved mountains, glistening waterfalls and ancient primeval forests - that's what you expect to see in New Zealand. But I want to tell you about the real New Zealand, not just the glossy photobook impressions.

You don't have to be a static van in the middle of the boondocks to get the sense that, in New Zealand, you're a very long way from anywhere. New Zealand's biggest city, Auckland, is one of the most remote cities in the world. Across the country, there are vast swathes of national park between one town and the next. You just can't escape the isolation in New Zealand, and a remote van in the middle of nowhere makes an appropriate metaphor for New Zealand; small, isolated and as eccentric as a flightless parrot.

Be under no illusions though, living in the bush is not typical. I am about ten miles as the crow flies from the nearest town and I am not representative of Kiwi life. You may have a sense of people living in a great, vast, unspoiled land, navigating the lonely trail up mountain crevices and dodging sheep as part of their daily commute. The reality, however, is quite different.

Monday 16 June

"New Zealand is a great country," I'd been told. "So long as you're bringing up your kids, retired, or visiting for your holidays.

But everybody else…you can go stir crazy, and want to get the hell out of here as quick as you can."

My local town, Paraparaumu, was filled with those who couldn't escape - pregnant teenagers doomed to spend their youth shouting at e-number fuelled toddlers, as they hurtled across the Coastlands shopping mall, threatening to knock over the blue rinse brigade like tenpins. Elderly women with impeccably permed hair spent their days endlessly perusing the shops and cafes, and sifting through the cut-price garments. It was as if the zombie classic Day of the Dead had been remade by the cast of Last of the Summer Wine. Even the automatic doors were arthritically slow. Often I had to be careful not to hit my head on the door while trying to escape the wretched place.

The town's main redeeming feature is it's library. A modern glass box of a building, filled with natural light and neat shelves of books, it might have been flung from the 23rd century. It's certainly an unexpected sight, this chunk of airy modernism, overlooking scrubland of long tussock grass and gangly legged pukeko birds. Intricate Maori carvings frame the entrance and each morning, one of us has the responsibility of raising the Union Jack, something I haven't been asked to do since I left the boy scouts.

The Maori origins of Paraparaumu literally translate as "scraps from the oven", referring to a warring party who arrived in the area long ago and discovered that the inhabitants had already fled, leaving behind nothing but the scraps of their meals. There are still plenty of scraps to be found in Paraparaumu, scattered among the concrete, but these days they are mostly polystyrene Burger King cartons and empty Coke cans. Marooned a mile away from the sea, Paraparaumu is a pretty typical Kiwi town and a sharp contrast to my eccentric home in the hills. Paraparaumu seems little more than an extended shopping centre, filled with identikit concrete and glass enclosed shopping outlets. The town was built in the 1960s, as were many small New Zealand towns. It was an ambitious age - everything built out of concrete, a place where people no longer walked, but drove. One can only hope that the town planners meant well at the time, but what they created was quite dreadful.

The town is filled with a vast expanse of car parks. I quickly discovered that it's physically impossible to walk into the Coastlands shopping centre without taking your life in your hands - dodging the family wagons and utes as they compete for parking space. And that's not the only problem. It's not like New Zealand is a country lacking in vast national parks. So why was there hardly a single patch of greenery in the whole town? Not one single park bench where you can sit during a sunny lunch hour, and enjoy the weather. The town had clearly never been planned, more likely it had been thrown up by a cement mixer.

We are surrounded by farms full of healthy, locally produced organic food, but there were no food markets in Paraparaumu and very few good places to eat out. Apart from a decent cafe and one curry house, ran by a local Fijian family, your choice is limited to McDonalds, Pizza Hut or KFC. Each one of them providing a limited selection of artery clogging deep-fried fat, sugar and starch. The only vegetable to be found was the lonely gherkin, which can't contribute much to your five a day. In their defence, perhaps the local council is finally recognising that their town is lacking a few essential ingredients. A public commission is afoot, to ask local residents how their home town could be improved. I submitted my own form, suggesting they evacuate the town, phone the White House to inform them that Osama Bin Laden was hiding in Paraparaumu's Pak'n'Save and wait for the United States Air Force to bomb the place flat. It would have been a small mercy.

End of diary entry

There is something of a myth surrounding New Zealand. It's not all scenic waterfalls, fern lined rivers, picturesque mountains and happy sheep, although I can't vouch for the sheep, they're quite inscrutable creatures. As for the scenery, they offer tourists "100% Pure NZ". Don't get me wrong, there is plenty of amazing scenery here, but I'm not sure you can call it "pure". Our national parks may be vast and beautiful, but they're full of introduced species, along with many paths and roads running through them. And these national parks aren't the real New Zealand because people don't live there - they live in towns, great big grey towns in suburban homes with privet fences.

Back in the day when I was a travelling van, I passed through most of New Zealand - the great wild outdoors, as well as the towns and cities. Almost every small town looks identical to the next, and yet they all lay claim to some spurious unique selling point to distinguish themselves from their identikit neighbours. The lengths some towns go to set themselves apart from one another will never cease to amaze me.

There was one small backwater by the name of Rolleston, an evocative and terrible place to park up. A derelict sign stood next to the petrol station, and tumbleweed may have blown across the street. The sign optimistically claimed Rolleston to be "The Town of the Future". Consisting of one small dairy shop, a weather beaten petrol station and little else, the town was a run-down lonesome place. Rolleston had definitely seen better days. At least for its own sake, I hoped it had. There was little to recommend, and it was hard to imagine how anyone could have considered Rolleston to be "The Town of the Future". Unless of course, the local council had overdosed on JG Ballard novels and decided that the future was going to be an apocalyptic wasteland, and had consequently designed Rolleston to fit in perfectly.

The township of Fielding claimed with pride to be the "Tidiest town in New Zealand", a commendable if uninspiring announcement. I waited patiently there for two slow weeks. My high point was having six weeks of dust and dirt track washed off of me. Unfortunately, my washing down was an intervention by the locals, because I was "lowering the tone of the campsite". Bloody cheek! Taihape has more imagination, and proudly has a giant gumboot standing outside the town as a constant reminder that they host New Zealand's annual boot throwing event. The idea is to throw a boot as far as you can manage, some participants apparently achieving a distance of hundreds of feet. I know you have to make your own entertainment in small rural towns, but really? I was less than impressed when one rogue boot flew across the car park and cracked my favourite window.

Some towns, like the "futuristic" Rolleston, are rather less successful. Indeed, there are entire towns which have been abandoned altogether. The tiny lost town of Cass in the centre of the South Island stands surrounded by remote mountain valleys amid white wispy clouds. Its few buildings in ruins, the rest destroyed, I find it hard to imagine that Cass once had a healthy population of around eight hundred. Cass is now no more than a ghost town, its population long since moved on to somewhere a little less remote and barren. All, that is, except for one man. A serious game hunter, Barry, is the last remaining inhabitant of Cass. More commonly known as Rambo, Barry spends his days isolated from the world, busily tracking and hunting, Rambo seems quite content in leaving the twenty-first century behind to live in quiet isolation. He's more tricky to spot than the extinct moa, but he can be found one day a year when the blokes from the railway come to Cass. They travel in for the annual cricket tournament, and enjoy a few beers before leaving Rambo alone again.

Another nearby ghost town, Otira, has been virtually destroyed by the electrification of the rail track, leaving its population of rail workers redundant. Standing virtually empty for many years, the entire town - including the pub - was purchased recently by an enterprising soul for the modest sum of $70,000. Since then, its buildings have been renovated amidst a national campaign to repopulate the community. One house had been bought by a reputable New Zealand painter and converted into an art gallery. Though you have to wonder how many intrepid art aficionados will make the long trip all this way to view his paintings - maybe he's shy about showing his work.

Most New Zealanders dwell in cities, if not in the towns. I've never loitered long in cities, I don't much care for concrete. Besides, the feeling is mutual. The metropolis doesn't have much time for a wandering caravan, as confirmed by the stack of unpaid parking tickets behind my sofa. These cities, in particular on the South Island, tend to closely resemble the homes from where the homesick pioneering Brits had fled. I've lost count of the number of times I've heard people remark that Dunedin is New Zealand's attempt at Scotland. I've never made it to Scotland and it's unlikely I ever will, but apparently if you turn the world upside down and shake a spare Scottish city loose from the British Isles, and drop it into the South Pacific, Dunedin is the result.

I never forgave Dunedin when a mechanic jacked me up to check a wheel and promptly stubbed his cigarette out on me. Incidentally, Dunedin is Gaelic for Edinburgh. The red brick buildings provide the city with a distinctive Scottish character, particularly in Dunedin train station, a sturdy landmark constructed of coarse black volcanic rock from the North Island. It's been said that Dunedin was designed and planned some twelve thousand miles away in Edinburgh, by people who had never once set foot in Dunedin and didn't have much of a map. If true, that explains a lot. They meant well, but they'd no idea what sort of geography this new city might be sitting on. They weren't to know that Dunedin has hills and not just any hills, but ludicrously steep ones, which is how Baldwin Street became the steepest street in the world. Trust me, it's a precarious drive for any vehicle, one careless slip of the handbrake and it's a one-way trip down this suburban ski-jump.

Christchurch, meanwhile, is great sprawl of leafy suburban streets and church spires puncturing the horizon. Jon says it looks a bit like Oxford or Cambridge. There is even a River Avon, complete with chaps in straw hats and punting boats for hire. But he says it doesn't feel like England at all, and apparently it's more like a bargain basement version of Las Vegas, where recreating Venice, Egypt and the like has become something of an obsession. Nevertheless, the average Kiwi prefers to live in these strange replica cities and bland towns, and would struggle to imagine why anyone would want to live anywhere else, least of all a van in the woods. They don't know what they're missing.

Turn the clock back and with some imagination, all these towns and cities were once dense with trees, remote and wild. Even New Zealand's largest city, Auckland, with its high-rise towers and the sort of traffic congestion that would make any international city proud, was once a backwater of sparse scrubland, unpopulated and overgrown with towering kauri trees. In 1840, when the 350 tonne Platina sailed into the harbour, all these lands were wop-wops, the back of beyond. Taking up most of the storage of the Plantina was the new residence of the Governor Captain William Hobson, a pre-fabricated building called a Manning Frame House. The pre-fab may be a step up from the five sticks and a blanket that some resorted to, but it was still essentially a wobbly box made of thin wood – pretty much a van without wheels.

Auckland is now home to almost half of the entire country's population, and there's a sharp division between those who live there and those in the rest of the country. A ruddy faced sheep shearer once hitched a ride with me to visit her sister in Auckland, and she best summed up the matter. She looked like she had birthed a few lambs in her time and her husband was a champion sheep shearer. "Aye, there's not so many sheep these days," she shrugged. "Used to be they outnumbered us forty-to-one, now its only ten-to-one," she explained, rolling her vowels. "We've a mixed herd, a few thousand mereeeeno, but since the price of wool crashed a few years back, there's no money in breeding sheep anymore." She tutted at the prospect of visiting Auckland.

"Auckland? Ah! Those city folks, they're not New Zealanders," she scalded. "All their money and fancy bars, looking down on the rest of us. They wouldn't know how to milk a cow if they tried!"

Wednesday 25 June

Almost every local I've met has considered my lifestyle to be dangerously foolish, or just plain mad. The more curious people ask me what brought me to live in the wop-wops. Did I not feel lonesome? Was I not afraid? Is it not cold in that caravan in the woods? "Why don't you just rent a flat?" they'd ask, on hearing I was living with no heating, with winter fast approaching. "You don't want to be living in the bush. The wop-wops is for animals and tramping, not living in!" I quickly learnt that while the locals might enjoy the great outdoors their country provides, spending the weekend fishing, zorbing down hills or running marathons over active volcanos, they wouldn't dream of living there.

I was surprised to discover that nearly everyone considered my living in the bush to be akin to moving several steps down the evolutionary ladder. The whole concept was almost offensive, as if I'd asked an Icelandic if they lived in an igloo, or someone from Dorset if they lived in a mud hut. Many would rather distance themselves from their unrefined pioneering past. "We don't all live in huts and caravans, y'know!"

I would try to explain the simple benefits of life in the wop-wops. How each morning started with a zing, especially the first hour or so when I woke up. In the absence of curtains, the sun welcomed itself in and basked my face in warmth. A supremely comfortable way to start the day, and a vast improvement on the harsh buzz of an alarm. I'd explain how the basic elements of survival came easily and conveniently. The sun was my heating system, promptly switching itself on at dawn before dialling down its warmth before nightfall. I hardly felt I needed a shelter at all – I'd gone native.

During the late eighteenth and early nineteenth centuries, a number of European settlers, castaways and convicts turned their back on civilisation. They were often Pakeha Maori, white Europeans who embraced Maori life. To Europeans, such people were renegades who had chosen savagery and rejected progress, law and order. Some two hundred years later, I felt a certain empathy with these outsiders, since most New Zealanders viewed my home in the wop-wops with a similar disdain.

I couldn't understand people's incredulous questioning at my choice to live in the bush, and I hadn't been prepared for it. My naive impression of Kiwi life had been largely influenced by an old Alan Whicker TV programme about New Zealand's hippy communities, featuring crystal healing and ear empowering with Hopi candles. Apart from a few leaflets for yogic retreats, the communities of colourful caravans and alternative lifestyles seemed to have all but vanished.

Have people grown so used to living a conventional way of life that they'd forgotten about the alternatives? For me, living something of a primitive and frontier life on the edge of civilisation serves to distill life down to the simplest components, which helps to work out what is really important and what is not. What did I really need? Food, shelter, clothing and fuel. That's all, I figured, casting away a great many things that are generally considered necessary or desirable.

Both my parents grew up under the shadow of the Second World War, with a make do and mend philosophy. I expect that more than a little of that attitude has rubbed off

on me. Take clothes for instance; I could
fill the van with fine threads, jackets and
trousers to wear and impress my neighbours
and colleagues. I could while away my spare
time choosing these garments. But to what
ends? Now that I'm living in the outback,
practical considerations became the most
apparent. Something warm to wear as the
nights grew cold, to retain my heat, and to
protect my legs from low branches and plants
– that would do me just fine.

I'd grown up wearing hand-me-downs from
cousins, and clothes were passed from family
to family. I was loathed to retire any of my
current clothes until they'd fallen apart,
and wouldn't buy any new ones until they
did. In fact I'd purposefully bought my most
wretched old clothes with me, so I could
bumpkin around them in the wop-wops before
throwing them out when I leave. The whimsical
fads of fashion are not for me – I'll save my
time and money for other pursuits. Besides,
many of these clothes are manufactured by
desperate people in terrible conditions. In
a world of diminishing resources, I like to
think that the trampiest hobo has the moral
edge over the dedicated follower of fashion.

And what of my shelter? No garage... No
second bedroom... My only toilet and bathroom
a sheer hike away in the woods... Without
any hot water. You might be surprised by
the things you don't miss. My home is like
a step back in time. I imagine that the
grand chronology of homes and housing works
something like this: cave > wattle and daub >
stone and tiles > bricks > glass and concrete.
Where's the humble caravan in all of this?

My home is more like those fashioned from branches and mud, hewn from the forest than a home of brick – and none the worse for it. Anyone lucky enough to find a friend or sympathetic fellow with a lump of land could easily live in such a place, relatively free from rents or mortgages. If the alternative is a larger and more luxurious box in town that's prohibitively expensive and whose costs prevent you from really living and enjoying your life, then living in the bush is a preferable option – by a country mile.

Think about it; instead of a house with a 30 year mortgage, build your home with the price tag of two disused caravans and some wood from a local lumber yard. What savings to be made, since money that doesn't need to be spent won't need to be earned. Time to enjoy the view, to read and walk and really relax. But how many people would be content to live like this? Not so many it seemed.

One man who understood the simple life was Bill, custodian of Fyffe House. Built upon the excavated bones torn from the guts of harpooned whales, Fyffe House is the only surviving building from the whaling era of Kaikoura's history. Constructed in 1854, the white clapboard house has hardly been touched since. A ramshackle and deathly monument to the whaling industry, white disks of whale vertebrae poke out from supporting walls. A simple wooden bed stood upon bare floorboards, nineteenth century wallpaper peeling from the walls. A visitor's book detailed how the last permanent resident, an eccentric bachelor, died here in 1980. He'd lived in the house his whole life, growing up here as a child, and later eking out a simple life from fishing and beach-combing. In all his lifetime, he didn't seem to have made a single improvement to the place. I had a nagging suspicion that others looked on my own backwater home as being similarly peculiar. My God, was I in danger of ending up like him, a strange hermit with nobody but the fish for company?

I fell into conversation with Bill, the guy who looks after this place. We sat on the veranda, overlooking the harbour and enjoyed the breeze blowing in from the Pacific, as the house gently creaked around us. "So what brings you to New Zealand then?" asked Bill. I told him of caravans, and wop-wops and of my life in London twelve thousand miles away. Bill nodded and smiled. I was surprised. He appeared to understand instantly what had driven me to live in the bush. I felt that I'd met a kindred spirit who quite understood the satisfaction that comes from escaping the city for a simpler life. "So what brings you to Kaikoura?" I asked him. "Well, I grew up here," he explained, waving his arm across the harbour. "Settled down and married a local Maori girl. She's a descendant of Te Rauparaha y'know, back when he came over the Cook Strait and invaded the Ngai Tahu's territory. They still don't like to talk about it around here."

Sitting with the great-grandson in-law of the legendary Maori warrior, we chatted about the future of Kaikoura. "You should have seen this place a few years ago, it was in a terrible state. No work, no opportunities and then Bill Solomon persuaded a few local families to put their homes up for collateral to buy a twelve seater inflatable boat. We never looked back." The thousands of visitors to Kaikoura have provided an entire industry for the town, from hostels and hotels to cafes and restaurants. "We're even getting a new library to house Kaikoura's historical documents".

There were, however, concerns among some of Kaikoura's residents, and Bill feared that the town could become a victim of its own success. "We've only three or four thousand residents in Kaikoura, but in 1996 we were getting 200,000 visitors a year. Today we get close to a million. Local families who have lived here for generations are selling up their homes by the waterfront for redevelopment, pocketing the money and moving out of the area." Bill sighed. "I love this town, it's a beautiful place to live. I'd hate to see it go like Queenstown, just another soulless tourist trap."

The modernisation of Kaikoura from an obscure quiet backwater into a modern centre for tourism isn't without its casualties, but no-one wished to see Kaikoura return to how it was twenty years ago. Perhaps it's a small price to pay for a unique and arguably eco-friendly industry that has enriched the lives of Kaikoura's residents, to a degree the whalers could never have imagined. Still, I sympathised with Bill, as he looked out over the Pacific. "It's not all beer and skittles y'know" he shrugged.

End of entry

Those of us who exist outside of New Zealand's towns are known as bachs - the collective noun for the huts, sheds, disused railway carriages and lone caravans that live deep in the outback. One wag described a typical bach as "something you built yourself, on land you don't own, out of materials you borrowed or stole". That pretty much summed up my own existence, which I would modestly describe as a collision between a trailer park and a lumber yard. You won't find a bach in a town or city, a true bach can only be found situated on some remote beach or an inland forest.

The bach was an inexpensive way for a family to enjoy a break - by the seaside or in the countryside, far away from urban life. As the era of exploration passed into the history books by the middle of the twentieth century, middle class New Zealanders took to visiting the wop-wops for leisure.

We humble mobile homes proved especially popular. The earliest caravans began to appear on New Zealand roads in the early 1920s, at that stage often little more than a trailer with a canvas roof. One early brochure urged those to "Wander where you will, stay as long as you like, move on when you please...there's no thrill to equal carefree happy vagabonding". Caravanning appealed to the sense of freedom that had spurned their adventurous forebears to leave the Old Country during the last century. Clubs were set up, camping grounds proliferated and the caravan industry boomed, providing cheap holidaying for all. Sadly, it wasn't to last, and in May 1979 Prime Minister Muldoon slapped a 20% sales tax on caravans. Petrol prices had risen too. It was an apocalypse. The bubble burst and before long, we increasingly found ourselves off the road and converted into chicken roosts or like myself, into a more permanent bolthole in some wild corner.

The basic old bach is now vanishing too, and gradually being replaced by the modern holiday house - professionally built homes in line with the increasing affluence of modern New Zealand. It used to be pretty easy to occupy a tract of unused land. Someone with the hunger, stamina and inclination could drag a caravan off road, move into the bush and live off the land, hunting and fishing. But many of these places were reviewed and destroyed after a fateful disaster at Cave Creek, when a viewing platform collapsed in Paparoa National Park. Instead of turning a blind eye, the DoC forced these huts and shacks to comply with house-building codes and fire regulations. Living out in the wilderness is becoming all but impossible. I may be one of the last of my kind, but it hasn't always been like this.

Take Ross Webber, he lived on his own island, Puangiangi, in the outer Marlborough Sounds for 46 years. Although Ross makes Robinson Crusoe and Alexander Selkirk look like amateurs, this wasn't a chapter of New Zealand's pioneering past. He actually didn't leave the island until the 1990s, having spent his life butchering his own sheep, catching fish and brewing his own beer in near isolation. Then there was the Japanese tourist, Keiko Agatsuma, who lived in a cave on Stewart Island for years, surviving on shellfish and seaweed before the authorities deported her. Gerald Cover, the so called Hermit of the Herbert Range lived 1,300 metres above sea level, and a nine-hour tramp from the nearest town. He was as agile and self sufficient as a mountain goat, making his own medicine from local mountain plants and frequently dodging lightning bolts. But he too was cleared from his remote home in 1997.

We humble bachs and lone caravans still have our admirers though, including photographers such as Robin Morrison and writers like Keri Hulme who lives in a van and wrote the award winning The Bone People. Petone based painter Geoffrey Notman's works often feature caravans. The singer Jordan Reyne lives in a van. There are fewer distractions in an isolated space, and so we appeal to those who wish to meditate and create. Yet the surprising truth is that New Zealand's urban population has exceeded that of the rural population, since as far back as 1911. By the time we got to the 2001 Census, only two per cent of New Zealand's population lived in rural areas. People have almost utterly abandoned country life in favour of towns and cities.

I don't know how many of us are left, but safe to say I am a panda of sorts and am definitely on the endangered list. I have my loyal supporters who appreciate living in the wild, those who'd photograph me and display me in a gallery. But most New Zealanders don't have much time for an old mobile home in the woods.

Jon paints an idyllic impression of living here in the bush, but this lifestyle has its risks. Before Jon arrived, I'd been broken into twice in a few short months. Removed from the rest of the world, I'd felt perfectly safe and secure in my unorthodox patch of paradise. You can easily assume that you're safe from intruders when you're in the middle of nowhere. After all, who would bother to travel all the way out here to the wop-wops and up that broken dusty track, just to break into a caravan? I'm hardly likely be fitted out with the latest hi-tech goodies, easily stolen and sold on the black market.

Despite having little worth pinching and pocketing, a solitary mobile home is a ripe target for thieves. There is no-one here to raise an alarm, and no twitching curtain of a neighbour. The surrounding natural world provides something of a false sense of security. Even here in the wop-wops, you need some kind of security system. Motion sensors maybe? Don't be ridiculous. CCTV? You must be joking. Instead a lock and chain for my gate, which would at least prevent anyone from driving a van up here and filling it with tins of beans and books of poetry - which is about all I have to offer. It's a shame to have to resort to a padlock, but I guess heaven has its pearly gates, after all.

Sunday 29 June

I wasn't envious of the so called civilised
urban world around me. For the most part,
I was happy with the tranquility that my
isolated existence brought. I perched on the
edge of my bed, cracked open a bottle of
Monteiths beer and admired the view. There
was something quite captivating about that
glorious final hour of sunlight, when the
light makes everything glow with life before
the darkness comes.

It's not always so glorious though, as I was
reminded when I travelled through the town
of Punakaiki recently. Punakaiki receives
plenty of passing tourist traffic thanks
to the eroded limestone rocks that provide
a briefly exhilarating display during high
tide, as a blowhole shoots sea water several
feet into the air. The rock formations are
known as the pancake rocks due to their round
layered shape. It's all very impressive for
about twenty, let's be generous, maybe thirty
minutes. But there's not much else there and
like many rural places, it's not always an
easy place to live.

The local pub formed the hub of this
little community, serving up various things
battered and fried with chips. A small tin
box by the fireplace read simply "Punakaiki
Local Radio, please give generously". Fixed
to the wall, a framed newspaper article told
how a local girl, in a fit of depression,
had thrown herself from the cliffs near the
local rock formations. It must have been
a devastating event, especially for such
a small community. Travelling through and

visiting these out of the way scenic places may be interesting enough, but I do wonder what it's like to grow up or live here. For this poor girl, being stuck in the wop-wops had proven an ordeal too much to bear. In this warm autumnal night, it wasn't an emotion I could relate to, but I would learn soon enough as winter approached.

Whilst the weather remained warm and bright, I found my mood reflected the climate. After all, I was living in something like a landscape painting and as I drank my beer and peered out the window, the horizon was mine and mine alone. The view ahead featured four rounded foothills, with dense green forests of indigenous New Zealand trees. I didn't know the names of the different trees, but I could make out the different textures of the larger mature trees against their smaller counterparts. Some were the lighter colour of olives, others a deeper evergreen, and every shade between.

As the sun dipped below the hills, the light quickly shifted and drained from the horizon and within twenty short minutes, it was totally dark, the only light provided by the moon and the stars. In the absence of any light pollution, the view of the Milky Way was breathtaking, a dense spray of stars that swept overhead. At times, the sky sparkled like a well endowed diamond necklace And yet for some reason, I was always slightly relieved to step back into the relative comfort of the caravan.

End of diary entry

Makiriri
(translation: winter)

Thump! Thump! Bang! I was beaten violently, knocked back and forth. A whoosh of chilled air ripped through me as if I were made of paper. Old Man Southerly had come to visit. The strong southerly gale pounded me blow upon blow, my windows creaked and my walls flexed and warped so much that one heavily laden bookcase almost toppled over. If you've never a felt a southerly, then imagine an earthquake erupting with ice cold lava.

New Zealand's climate is influenced by two weather systems. Commonly known as the northerlies and the southerlies, northerly winds blow through from the South Pacific and tend to be warm and wet. Whereas southerly winds howl unrestrained across the Southern Ocean, straight up from the Antarctic. Old Man Southerly gives the impression of some slightly crazed elderly relative with a frosty glare, snowy white beard and cold hands. Why do they give the weather a name? Perhaps it's easier to tolerate a violent storm when it has a name, but still, I find it strange that people refer to this howling, freezing, Antarctic weather system as if it were an old friend that's come for tea and cake.

The temperature wasn't just falling; it was plummeting like a piano in a silent film. Winter was closing in. The southerly winds roared like some great beast, angry at the world, beating it into submission. By morning the gales relent, replaced by a softer, gentler natural form of music, the leaves gently coaxed to flutter in a chorus of natural symphony. I don't much care for being shaken like a cocktail, but it's more of a shock to Jon. He will have to get used to it, because Old Man Southerly likes to move in, put his feet up and make himself comfortably at home. The temperature is around zero, and it's no warmer indoors than outdoors.

For several consecutive nights, Old Man Southerly stomps about, knocking and bashing, freezing everything in his path. The first serious frost of the year arrives, and the scenery has the appearance of a Dickensian Christmas card. The morning dew hangs on the grass and forest and I am coated, walls and roof, in a layer of crunchy crystallised water. The lush green grass around me is bleached with tinges of white and blue. The scene is really rather picturesque. Fortunately the cold doesn't bother me too much, although I will suffer later with a touch of rot thanks to the damp.

There's no two ways of putting it - winter has arrived with an icy punch, and living in the wop-wops in a caravan is presenting all sorts of new challenges for Jon. I have no heating, my water pipes are about to freeze solid and he's cocooned in his bed much of the time, hibernating like some kind of feral animal. Worse still, I fear his unrestrained joy of living in the bush is fast disappearing.

Sunday 6 July

A freak snowstorm left a white frosting over the surrounding hills. My little corner of civilisation was transformed into one of those ornamental domes that's shaken to scatter the scenery in a flurry of snow. The radio reports that the area hasn't seen snow like it in a decade or more. Potholes in the road fill with rainwater and freeze solid overnight. The poor cows aren't faring any better either, standing nonchalantly in the neighbouring fields with a white coat of frost upon their backs.

Even staying indoors, my hands were numb with the cold so I locked up and struck north, with no real destination in mind, more intent on leaving than arriving. I refuse to abandon the caravan out of principle, but I do need to escape for a day or two. Four hours later I found refuge at a hostel in Whanganui.

Whanganui is a town with strong Maori roots and as with all Maori names, there are a particular set of rules to observe, if you're going to pronounce it properly. Needless to say, few go to the effort of getting it right. While I was working in the tongue-twisting town of Paraparaumu, my librarian colleagues initiated me in correct pronunciation of New Zealand place names – an absolute minefield, and none more so than Paraparaumu itself.

Before leaving London, a Kiwi colleague gave me some advice. "No-one actually says the full name Paraparaumu, if you want to fit in, you'll want to abbreviate it to Parapram", or as she put it "Parapraaaaaaaaiiiiiim!", emphasising the latter section of the word with a sharpness that sounded like nails being dragged across a chalkboard. Most people simply say "Paraparam", or the even more concise "Parapram", but a brave few attempt to pronounce their hometown fully, often ending up with "Para-para-ooo-moo", with short pauses in between each syllable. Through working for the local council, I discovered that even these attempts were not correct, and I learned to refine my "Para-prrrrr-au-moo", rolling the second "r" into the back of my mouth, and turning it into an "ow" or an "au" before finishing it off with a short "moo" or "mu". Although technically this was correct, I expect that of Paraparaumu's twenty thousand residents, perhaps as few as a hundred actually pronounce the place the way it was intended... And that's just Paraparaumu.

As a general rule of thumb, words and places that begin with "w" are pronounced "f". So, you might reasonably have thought Whanganui ought to sound like "Funganui", as in some kind of giant mushroom, but it doesn't. If anyone had pronounced it mushroom style in the past, then their way of saying Whanganui is long since gone and forgotten. This may seem like I'm splitting hairs, but there is often a great yawning chasm between how Maori pronounce place names and how Pakeha refer to these same places. Consequently, I could have a long conversation with someone before realising that we're actually talking about the same place.

As for Whanganui, I explored the town and went for a walk through Queens Park, pausing to admire the rather grand Neo-classical Sarjeant Art Gallery. The town had recently renovated many of its surviving colonial buildings, including the dramatic Victorian Opera House. Like some escapee from a Mark Twain novel, a paddle-steamer churned its way along the brown tinged Whanganui River. Known as the upside down river, its currents resemble a torrent of brown slurry. Yet a few brave souls have managed to dive beneath the muddy surface and discover the depths of the river, which are actually remarkably clear. Wanganui would prove to be a town with hidden depths.

While relaxing in the lounge munching pizza, I thought about how this everyday act felt like a luxury, since I don't have the benefits of an oven nor any chance of a delivery. I looked up and noticed that sitting opposite me was the most beguiling young woman. Her large dark eyes were watching me. A silver stud in her nose caught the light, contrasting against her dark complexion. She had a playful spark in her eye that utterly captivated me and I was immediately struck by her air of confidence.

Her name was Pania and she was a graphic design student at the nearby Massey University. "I work here and get my rent for free," she explained. "Well, cleaning the toilets and showers. Pretty scummy really." She shrugged. "But it's not so bad, I get to meet some interesting people," she commented, looking long into my eyes. "Well, I'm not very interesting," I replied. She disagreed and laughed. "I don't know. I've never met someone who lives in a caravan in the forest before…"

She'd noticed something about me that I hadn't. I had changed. I suspected Pania was intrigued, attracted even, to my unconventional existence in the van. I'd had a vague impression that backpackers in particular were captivated by my feral life in the back of beyond. I tried not to exaggerate my life, and I'd never described myself as a Tarzan or Mowgli figure. I didn't have the physical prowess of a hunter or an outdoors man. Nonetheless, I had acquired some kind of notoriety, which seemed to have a glamourising effect on some people. It might be what New Zealanders refer to as someone being "staunch", which isn't down to physical strength or fearlessness, although sometimes staunchness is misunderstood as such. Staunch is an attitude, walking directly through a crowd of people who will step aside for you. Maori have a very refined sense of this, and much of their history is dedicated to developing or respecting those with "mana", which roughly translates or can include influence, prestige and power. Despite the majority of locals viewing my wop-wops life with disdain, there were others, like Pania and many travellers who for whatever reason respected my strange life.

The hostel came equipped with a games room, complete with a threadbare pool table and a dart board that'd been punctured repeatedly over the years. A few of us played a game of Killer, taking turns to knock one another off of the darts board. Inexplicably, my darts kept puncturing my new friend's slice of the board, and before long and quite by accident I had expelled her from the game. Charmingly, she stamped her foot and crossed her arms. "Jon, how could you!" she pouted, admonishing me for my cruel behaviour as I protested my innocence. We chatted through to the small hours about everything and anything, but I do remember that she had some clout with the local iwi, the Maori community. In short, a friend from college had told Pania that her handbag had been stolen. Based on her friend's description of the culprit, Pania had "had words" with some of her Maori contacts. Word was put to the street, and not before long the handbag had mysteriously returned to its owner.

The following day, we walked together to the local chippy around the corner. Sheltered from a torrential downpour, we sat upon the bench outside and pulled apart a whole roast chicken with our greasy fingers. Pania was fearless and funny. The chicken was devoured as we laughed over our unlikely romantic meal. Our arms linked as we hopped carefree over the puddles down the street. "You want some?" she offered, handing me a new flavour of chewing gum. Popping one into my mouth, I somehow managed to temporarily glue my lips together. Her eyes lit up as she laughed. I couldn't remember the last time I had enjoyed myself with such abandon.

End of diary entry

I'm pleased for him because frankly he could use a little company. You can't spend your whole life cooped up in a caravan in the woods. Besides, he's opened a door into an aspect of New Zealand life that I can't provide.

Jon has filled the kettle and to fill the silence, put the radio on for some company and a thread of civilisation. All is dark outside now, as the winter gales rattle him around me like a marble in a can.

"A building site in Paraparaumu recently lifted a ban preventing women entering the construction site," announced the local news. The local iwi, Te Ati Awa ki Whakarongotai, had secured a contractors agreement that the site be men only. To the bemusement of many residents, Kapiti Council agreed to this, on the basis that Maori rights took precedent over women's rights. In the latest development the iwi were forced to concede, but claimed in their defence that it was an age old Maori custom and that "Women entering the site would get a swift kick in the bum!"

Does this sound extraordinary to you? Certainly, Jon was bemused. You might think the Maori's view a little old fashioned, but it's not uncommon for the local Maori community, or iwi, to be closely consulted on local issues. They're often asked to bless the construction of new public buildings, a process which may well be unique to New Zealand. You certainly wouldn't find this happening in Australia, or America. I think most would agree that relationships with the indigenous people haven't always been easy, but many New Zealanders are now becoming increasingly proud of their Maori roots. Well, mostly. As part of the radio report, politician Ken Shirley reflected one strand of public opinion, by commenting that if all Maori traditions were observed then "There would be a human sacrifice on the construction site, and the workers would be banned from having sex until the building is completed." I don't suppose he gets invited to rub noses with the locals too often.

The Maori backstory might shed a little light on these traditions and customs. I'm a caravan, not a historian, but I've heard and read enough to give you the gist of it. They are the descendants of East Polynesian explorers, who arrived to settle New Zealand during an era of widespread Polynesian exploration in the 13th century AD. Until then, no-one else had lived in New Zealand or is likely to have discovered it. It's truly remarkable that throughout 10,000 years of history, humankind had explored and settled in almost every habitable continent in the world, including Australia. But New Zealand remained one of the very last places to be colonised.

The Polynesians were outstanding explorers and settled a vast area across the Pacific, as far north as Hawaii, all the way to Easter Island and finally south to New Zealand. Take a moment to look at a globe or map - it's larger than you think. But New Zealand was quite unlike anywhere else that they'd discovered. It was larger for a start, bigger than all the other Polynesian islands put together: some – 1,600 kilometres from tip to toe, with 18,000 kilometres of coastline. Temperatures varied much more wildly, too. These Polynesians would adapt and change their life to suit the conditions and climate, because having discovered this new home, there was no going back. The strange thing is, no one has found any evidence of contact after the initial settlement. A long way from home, these explorers never returned and over time became Maori, isolated and evolving quite separately to their Polynesian ancestors.

The local fauna and flora influenced what the settlers grew and ate, along with what types of homes they built and lived in. They had to learn quickly how to survive in this new world. The abundance of land and resources in New Zealand led to larger populations, plus greater opportunities to refine their skills. A new mineral, greenstone, allowed the development of more detailed and intricate carvings. The fibres of the local New Zealand flax enabled more elaborate clothing and textiles. And all of these qualities went on to become distinctly Maori.

The more I think about it, the more I realise that isolation has come to define every aspect of New Zealand life, and the Maori are no exception. As with the wildlife before them and the European colonists who would follow centuries later, a distinct microcosm of culture had came about. The Maori way of life is so unusual largely thanks to New Zealand being so far from the original Polynesian lands that had been left behind; a prime example of the wop-wops effect yet again.

Thursday 24 July

Before I left London, I'd wondered if I might get cold in the caravan so I'd attempted to mentally prepare myself. Last winter, I had switched off the heating. Did this frosty

ordeal prove to be much help? No, not really.
I was cold then and I'm freezing now.

The following morning, a consecutive heavy
frost had proved too much for my nearby
bathroom. Surrounded by steep forested
hills, the ground was barely touched by the
warmth of sunlight. The pipes had now frozen
solid. Only a few short weeks ago, I barely
had a drop of water because of the drought.
Ironically, now the water is plentiful
and it's quite beyond my reach. My only
respite from living like some sort of feral
creature was the shower facilities at work.
My librarian colleagues were far too polite
to say, but I can't have made for a pretty
picture as I shivered into work each day and
tried to avoid leaving a trail of dirt behind
me, leading to the bathroom facilities. My
attitude to work had also changed; instead
of being bored when stamping and cataloguing
books, I was only too glad to have somewhere
warm and dry to sit for a few hours. There
was no other way of putting it; life at
the caravan had changed dramatically. It was
no longer a pleasure, but something to be
endured.

I locked up my increasingly frost bitten
home and take to the road. For a change, I
take a short detour and within moments, a
freight train roared past the bonnet of my
car at tremendous speed, thundering along
the tracks with a typical click and a clank.
I'd almost not spotted it at all. I'd never
taken this particular route before - despite
being a short drive from the caravan and
one left turn from the Maungakotukutuku
road. There was no traffic signal to manage

the traffic, no barrier to prevent someone crossing the track. There'd only been a small sign indicating the train tracks ahead. I'd thought there are so few trains running along this route, I'd been half inclined to just cross it with a casual glance. Fortunately my sense of self preservation had trumped my cavalier attitude and I had slammed my right foot on the brake. I exhaled deeply. My heart beat with a fast rhythm in time with the accelerating train ahead. Finally, the train passed and with great care, I put the car in first gear and if it is possible for a car to tip-toe, then I tip toed across the track.

I arrived to discover Pania up to her elbows in rubber marigolds, cleaning the hostel. She pursued me around the hostel, waving her dirty rubber gloves towards me. "Have they been where I think they've been?" I asked, as I ran up a flight of stairs. "Of course," she shouted in hot pursuit, laughing as I scrambled into a bathroom and bolted the door.

That evening we played a few games of pool at the hostel, with an increasingly drunken Kiwi and a pair of stoical German backpackers. "Yeah, I've been to the South Island," announced Kiwi Bloke, joining in with the travel banter. "I went to Picton for the day. Had a few beers and got the next ferry home." This wasn't unusual. Despite being a nation of travellers, I'd noticed that New Zealanders who'd travelled around their own country were few and far between. Wild, remote New Zealand might be the marketing pitch to Europeans, but this landscape is of limited interest to the typical local, who are more interested in the cities of Europe and America. Maybe people always want what they can't get, thinking that the grass is always greener.

Upon hearing my story of living in a remote caravan in the bush, Kiwi Bloke snorted with laughter. "Sounds bloody awful mate, no heating and no telly?" He wasn't entirely wrong. Winter was bloody awful in a caravan with no heating, but since he hadn't experienced it, he hadn't earned the right to make judgement. I let the comment pass, well used to the disdain. The backpackers were in awe though, insisting that I was experiencing the real New Zealand, much to the annoyance of Kiwi Bloke who downed his beer with a thump. Realising he was losing at pool, Kiwi Bloke generously insisted on paying for a taxi, whisking the five of us out for a night on the tiles in Whanganui.

Our first stop was The Grand. It didn't seem particularly grand though, consisting of a long bar, stripped of atmosphere and filled with bright tube lighting and pokey machines. The tables were sticky and crowded with pitchers of beer. Getting in a round of Speight's Gold Medal Ale, we made for the backroom, where a covers band enthusiastically mutilated Hendrix and Rolling Stones songs. A big burly fella with a strong resemblance to Peter Jackson's slightly fatter, older, brother wobbled with enthusiasm and air guitared across the dance floor. We claimed a corner and danced, whilst simultaneously fending off the drunken revelry around us. There was an unusual assortment of age groups in the club. Middle aged types threw their hair around to Meatloaf covers, and a younger crowd propped up the bar while bickering over whose pint had been spilled. That's the thing about a night out in a small town, you can sometimes feel like you're gate crashing a stranger's wedding reception.

The night progressed and we moved on to Whanganui's premiere nightspot, the western themed and luridly named Slippery Saddle. Inside, the floor heaved with a mass of bodies, dancing, bouncing and bumping into one another, as everyone competed for a few more square inches in which to move. Above the bar, a life-sized mannequin of a cowboy was lying on his back, grasping an empty bottle of beer, as a pre-programmed computer knocked out a mish mash of contemporary dance versions of classic disco hits. No-one seemed to mind about the terrible music, jumping around as if they were having the time of their lives, pickling themselves with plastic cups of beer and Bacardi Breezers. A friend of Pania's put on a lively floor performance to the Proclaimers I Will Walk 500 Miles. In the style of a knee-jigging Cossack, he dropped to the floor, kicking his legs energetically out from beneath him. It was quite something. After all, it's not every day you see a man perform a traditional Russian dance to a Scottish song, on an island in the South Pacific.

I couldn't afford to be distracted though, as I was keeping my eye on Kiwi Bloke who was manoeuvering towards Pania. Staggering through the throng with another generous round of plastic cups of beer, he leaned over and slurred in my ear, "Meet, sheeee's a beeeet of alreeeght!" with a knowing wink, and a stagger. "Is she, y'know, WITH you?" I politely warned him off and unperturbed, Kiwi Bloke lurched away, approaching a tall blonde who told him where to go in no uncertain terms.

The following morning we took a drive out of town to visit the scenic Virginia Lake. Admiring the scenery, I called her a duck, and she told me I was a cabbage. I don't know why, but it sort of made sense at the time with my arms wrapped around her, holding her close. She pressed herself against me. Her long eyelashes brushed lightly, tickling my face. "Y'know if Lionel knew about you," she breathed warmly into my ear, "he would come after you and slice you up into little bitty pieces." Oh, I thought, loosening my grip just a little.

Lionel was a chef and semi-permanent guest at the hostel, with an impressive selection of professional kitchen knives. He was a friendly if burly looking Kiwi who'd taken upon himself the role of Pania's protector. He took me to one side. "Look at my lovely knives" he said, running his thumb along the flat of the blade. "I know you won't do anything to upset Pania, will you." It wasn't a question, and I was well aware that I'd have to be careful. Not only was there a knife-wielding chef to consider, I also couldn't overlook the connections she had at the local iwi that saw stolen bags mysteriously reappear. Not only that, but her cousin lived in the room next door to her. If we weren't very careful, word could easily get back to her family. I was told that her folks weren't, how shall we say, entirely comfortable with their daughter being a modern independent woman.

The weekend flew by and before returning to the caravan, we took a short walk along the wide murky expanse of the Whanganui River and arrived in Moutoa Gardens. There stood, or at least once stood, an unfortunate statue of a local statesman. Apart from the stone plinth, all that remained of him was a pair of feet, broken at the ankle "Did he have famous feet?" I asked foolishly, looking at the victim of a terrifying sculptural punishment beating. Pania looked at me incredulously, and explained that Moutoa Gardens had been the site of a historic Maori protest over land rights and had been occupied for several months. The event had been peacefully abandoned, but had left lasting acrimony amongst both the Maori and Pakeha communities. Nobody appeared to be in a hurry to re-attach the statue to his feet.

End of diary entry

Jon has stumbled into the sharp end of New Zealand politics, facing the key question of who owns the land. Everything rests on a single document that was written and signed in the distant past of 1840. The Treaty of Waitangi established British sovereignty over New Zealand and bestowed equal rights on all citizens, Maori, and Pakeha (that is non-Maori, and predominantly British settlers). The Crown stepped in as sole purchaser of Maori land to prevent unscrupulous settlers buying Maori land for the price of a few magic beans – in theory, at least.

Almost two hundred years later, you can hardly hear a radio or see a newspaper without mention of the treaty.

It has a profound impact on society - what benefits you're eligible for, who owns the beaches, and even the portrayal of the heritage of their humble lone caravan.

Jon went to Wellington to see the treaty for himself. New Zealand's founding document is now kept safe and secure in its own environmentally controlled vault, surrounded by twelve inches of steel. The power and influence of this document over the country can hardly be underestimated, yet he'd noted his surprise at its miserable condition. Neglected in every sense, the treaty has been ignored, mistreated, and left to rot, its raggedy edges visibly nibbled by hungry rodents. I can empathise to some degree, as I know how it feels to have a rodent give me a good gnawing.

The Treaty of Waitangi was signed, voluntarily and without threat or duress by several hundred Maori chiefs across the country. According to Jon's notes, the signatures on the ageing parchment were still visible. Those from the Bay of Islands who'd had the most European contact had legibly inscribed their name in English. Tribes from the South Island were represented with a simple cross or pictogram of waves or circles that represented the chief's moko, their elaborate facial tattoos. Unsurprisingly, the agreement proved controversial from the outset. Why? Well, what do you expect when there are two versions of the treaty. One was written in English with twenty-four signatures, the other in Maori which was signed by 526 tribal leaders, the Maori version being the true and legally binding version of the treaty. Needless to say, the two treaties are quite different. One particular discrepancy has been the differing definitions and interpretations of "sovereignty". Maori tribal leaders saw themselves as self-governing, with the British Monarch performing a purely ceremonial role. In contrast, the British ultimately saw the treaty as a means to extend their Empire. Between 1831 and 1881, some 400,000 emigrants relocated to New Zealand, irrevocably changing the nature of the country.

Two very different worlds collided, as settlers branched out and sought more land. When it came to land ownership, you might say the Maori tribes had more in common with the Native Americans than the European settlers. Traditionally, land was owned collectively by the tribe, based on the inheritance of their ancestors or conquest. Consequently an individual tribal leader did not have the right to sell or exchange land without the consent of his people. Yet some Maori chiefs sold tribal lands that were not theirs to sell, and in other cases, chiefs sold the lands of neighbouring tribes to undermine their rivals. Missionaries were among the first to purchase Maori land, and are said to have "Come to do good and did very well indeed". As far as I can tell, the sale of land was an unholy mess which was carefully exploited by Crown representatives and European settlers, all in total breach of the Treaty of Waitangi.

The consequences of these land purchases continue to reverberate through New Zealand society to this day. Compensation is provided to those who claim Maori ancestry, in an attempt to make amends for generations of discrimination. But sadly, poverty remains widespread among the Maori. Life expectancy is eight years less for Maori than that of other New Zealanders and two out of five Maori have no educational qualifications whatsoever. New Zealand has more people in what is termed substandard property than most of the rest of the developed world. And yes, I am embarrassed to say that caravans are considered substandard. In the past, the humble Kiwi motor home might have been an affordable holiday location. But for the less affluent, a caravan, especially a lone van like me, is instead synonymous with poverty and hardship.

According to the radio, we're experiencing the coldest winter in several years. As I said, It makes little difference to me, I'm just a caravan after all. But Jon is far less resilient, with only a solitary single bar electric heater to huddle around for comfort and warmth. The little heater fights a brave battle. After all, it has valiantly prevented my windows from freezing entirely. But to put things into perspective, the temperature is so low in the kitchen that when Jon went to put milk in his tea, big chunks of ice cubes dropped into the mug, frozen like an unappetizing slush puppy.

What he's missing is the dry, crackling warmth of a log fire. Ironically, I have a wood burning stove and there's plenty of dead wood around. The problem for Jon is that the wood is soaked through and beyond use, and the wood burner has a post-it sticker on the chimney clearly stating "Do not use!". In different circumstances Jon would be snug and cosy, with a hearty fire to warm his bones and cheer his spirits. Alas, I'm built out of thin panels of light processed wood which would burn as fast as kindling. In fact I would probably burn to the ground in a few short minutes, which is only part of his exasperating problem. The surrounding forest is under the protection of the local council. No open fires are permitted. No bonfires, no wood burning stoves and no log fires. No wonder he's cold.

Friday 1 August

Each day in the caravan felt colder than the last. Like clockwork, every morning began with thick heavy clouds and a concrete grey sky. The southerly winds continued to blow and roar through like some great beast, angry at the world, beating me into submission. I didn't so much leave the van as flee. Besides, it's not every day you get the opportunity to visit a marae, but Pania had worked her charm with great success.

The marae is the heart of a Maori community, with tremendous prestige and spiritual value, and it is in these buildings that tribal issues are discussed and deliberated. Marae buildings are often to be found overshadowed by shopping precincts, office blocks and housing estates. The distinctive triangular

A-frame structure of a marae is a familiar landmark in most towns around the North Island and as far south as Christchurch.

A short ceremony was necessary before I was permitted to enter. "Have you visited a marae before?" asked a woman in a floral dress who appeared to be in charge. I'd been to the themed Tamaki Brothers tour in Rotorua, but I wasn't sure whether that counted. This marae was the real deal, the living, working heart of the local Maori community. "You'll be invited into the marae with a powhiri, formally welcoming you," she explained. "You will need to stand next to your woman to defend her, until a karanga is called, inviting you to enter." I knew that I wouldn't last long in the face of a full tribal attack, but fortunately the large wooden gate swung open and a blow from a conch signalled our entrance.

Surrounding the familiar meeting house, there were other buildings scattered about, in between native trees and statues of mythological characters. The local Maori were dressed in smart casual clothes, rather than the traditional woven flax of their ancestors, serving as a reminder that this was not an artificial tourist experience. Instead, we were guests being invited into someone's home. Visitors to a marae are still expected to donate a gift, or "kohe", as is the custom. Traditionally this might have included food or textiles, such as flax baskets. Our host for the day, Hugh Grace, was a stocky fella with a little grey around the edges. He introduced himself and explained that although bartering and gifts were common in his ancestor's days, the Maori since moved with the times. "These days we prefer our kohe to be hard currency," he laughed, "exchangeable at all good supermarkets and Pak'n'Saves across the country."

We removed our shoes and placed them on the sheltered entrance to the meeting house, before following Hugh into the building. "Do you know why we remove our shoes?" Hugh asked. I shook my head. "Apart from the tribes of Rotorua," Hugh explained, "every marae across the country expects visitors to remove their shoes before entering the meeting house. It's symbolic and means that you are paying respect to your hosts. The area you just walked through in front of the meeting house is called the marae atea and represents Tumatenga, the God of War. The meeting house we are sitting in represents Rongo, the God of Peace." Hugh illustrated our surroundings with a wave of his arm. "The timber supports are his spine and arms. By removing your shoes, you ensure that no trace of war is brought inside and that the talks between the tribes can be conducted in a civil manner." I'd been wondering about that. "Plus it keeps the floor clean", he joked. Hugh revealed that he was a member of the Council of Elders, so he was allowed a voice on any number of subjects for discussion at the marae; ranging from betrothals, feuds and celebrations, to co-ordinating with the local council over local issues such as the environment and education.

"My ancestry, my whakapapa is from the east coast, near Gisbourne. I settled here thirty years ago to be here with my wife. I've always been treated well and accepted as a member of the iwi. I even attend the Council of Elders." Hugh's expression shifted. "But there are still times, especially during heated debates, when someone reminds me, 'Hugh, ye not from here, its not ye business, bro.'"

During such heated debates, Hugh had his own unique way of defusing the situation. "Instead of swearing and losing my temper, I just tell them 'Aroha mai ki Ahau' which means 'I love you'. They never know what to say to that, it puts them in their place." I reckon you'd have to know someone pretty well before you tried that tactic though. I wouldn't like to try that out down the pub on a lively Friday night.

Hugh asked whether I wanted any words translated in Maori. "I've been told Maori don't have any swear words, is this true?" I asked. It seemed unlikely. What would you say when your burnt your finger in the hangi, or stubbed your toe on the marae? Hugh looked a little sheepish. "Well, it's true. We don't really have any swear words, though the youngsters, they're using English swear words all the time." "I suppose," Hugh paused, "you could tell someone they're a pokokohua. But I would never say it myself and I don't know anyone who would... It would be a terrible thing to say." I was intrigued, but Hugh steadfastly refused to explain its meaning, clearly embarrassed by having mentioned it. Later, I looked the word up in a Maori-English dictionary and discovered that pokokohua literally meant boiled head. The strange insult refers to the act of cooking and eating another person's head, a practice eliminated by the arrival of the Christian missionaries. Maori tribes, like their Polynesian cousins, believed that the head embodied a person's soul. Eating an enemies head would not only devour them in this life, but also ruin their chances in the next life.

Hugh changed the subject. "Every time I hear the weather girl on the television, it makes me sad and angry to hear the places named by my ancestors. The pronunciation is abused by the Pakeha." There was a good reason for Hugh's keen attention to vocabulary. Hugh was a healer who used the traditional power of healing prayer to help the sick. If the language is not exactly precise, he explained, the prayers will simply not work. When all modern medicines had failed, Hugh would often be requested to visit a loved one's sick bed in the hope that he might conjure some miracle. "What do you do when your medicine doesn't work?" I asked. Our genial host faltered a moment before replying. "I've stood by the beds of desperately ill people, children even and sometimes I've been able to help them, when God permits it because He isn't ready to take them just yet. Other times, there's nothing I can do but clear the way for the first heaven, before their souls return to Hawaiki, our homeland."

Hugh led us outside the marae. "Every one of these trees has some medicinal purpose. Some of their leaves can be distilled to treat headaches, others for upset stomachs. Y'see over there," Hugh pointed, "the leaves from the evergreen Karangu shrub make a good poultice for healing broken bones and fractures, and these over here, Karama are sacred too, and very useful for the urinary system and women's problems." The knowledge of herbal medicines and treatments has been handed through countless generations, but Hugh was worried that these skills might die with him. "Many of the youngsters aren't interested," he explained. "They'd rather just go to the pharmacy and take an aspirin." Hugh's own teacher had been the revered Maori healer Alexander Philips, who was something of a legend among contemporary Maori healers. Philips claimed that prior to their arrival in the South Pacific, the Maori people were descended from the lost tribes of Israel, having travelled through South America. A dubious theory at best, but Hugh was a convert nonetheless.

"Mr Philips noticed the parallels between Aztec imagery and Maori carvings, and believed that our homeland Hawaiki was in fact Mexico. How else do you explain our having the kumara, sweet potato, an American staple? In 1990 he set out on an expedition to Mexico City and Chile, to investigate this theory for himself. No sooner had Mr Philips arrived in Mexico City Airport, than an old Mexican woman approached him, speaking to him in fluent Maori. She'd never even heard of New Zealand." Taking it as a sign, Alexander Philips travelled into Chile and upon discovering that there had been a drought there for many years, the Maori healer lifted the spell, returning the rain clouds to Chile. According to the story, Philip's taxi driver was in such a state of shock that he crashed his car. He'd never had to use his windscreen wipers before.

We took a break for lunch and tucked into cold cuts, sweet kumara potatoes and salad. I welcomed the change from stir fried vegetables and noodles in the caravan, or the usual take away fish'n'chips. "We're very sorry that we can't offer either of you a glass of wine or beer," one of the women apologised. "But many of our people have suffered from alcoholism so we took the decision to ban all alcohol from inside the marae."

I finished off my glass of feijoa juice, and Hugh returned to continue his introduction to Maori life. I was given a crash course in Maori history, in particular the King Movement, when back in the 1860s the increasing stress between European and Maori relations caused the Waikato Maori to unite and elect a Maori King. Until the arrival of the Europeans, the Maori people had no sense of nationhood. Instead, they were a disparate collection of tribes with their own lands, alliance and feuds. The term Maori itself was only coined after the arrival of Captain Cook. Quite literally, it translates as "normals" to distinguish the indigenous peoples from the so called European gentlemen: "rangatira Pakeha". The King Movement has continued to this day, although the current monarch is not a King, but a Queen and it's all a far cry from the pomp and luxury of British Royalty. Rather than live in a grand palace, the Maori Queen lives in a quiet wooden clapboard bungalow way out in the wop-wops, not so dissimilar to my own solitary caravan.

"Well, I guess I ought to teach you a waiata," Hugh suggested. "We always have a song for visitors. Many of our songs have been passed down through the generations and describe the history, myths and lives of our people." Hugh pulled out an acoustic guitar. "I know a guitar isn't strictly speaking a traditional Maori instrument, but we've been playing guitars for more than two hundred years now, ever since they arrived in these islands." A little self-consciously I sang along. "It's not as though, love was created now, was handed down by, our ancestors." I sang along with Pania, laughing and enjoying the moment.

The conversation took a darker turn. A terrible tragedy had struck this place not so long ago, in the very building in which we were sitting. A young Maori had hung himself from the rafters of the meeting house. Having never been accepted by his in-laws, his suicide was believed to be an act of revenge. His death had brought great shame upon the family, as well as being a difficult time for all concerned. Hugh had arranged for the boy's coffin to be placed beneath the scene of the suicide, rather than at the rear of the meeting house as was traditional, to cleanse the curse from the building. As the coffin was removed from the meeting house, young teenagers had shouted abuse at the bereaved family, and the funeral almost descended into a riot. The Council of Elders had physically restrained the various parties. On that sombre note, we called it a day and stepped outside into the sunshine.

End of diary entry

One sad fact about suicide is that the rates are far higher among the Maori than that of other New Zealanders. And perhaps in connection to this, gang membership and drug use is also higher among the Maori people. New Zealand has more gangs per head than almost anywhere else in the world, and they are responsible for much of the violent crime in this otherwise peaceful country. Some claim that there's a long line of Maori violence, dating all the way back to their first contact with the Europeans. A Dutchman called Abel Tasman was the first European to land in New Zealand. It was a brief and bloody encounter and he named the spot Murderers Bay when four of his men were killed.

A few hundred years later, I was sat in a caravan park outside Porirua when my tenant at the time, Ross, a Pakeha incidentally, returned late after a nights drinking. He was limping, his face heavily bruised and covered in dried blood. "What the hell happened to you?" asked his girlfriend, a little unsympathetically, I thought. "Blaady Mongrel Mob," he replied. "That's what happened." "We've just got back from the police station." he explained. "Been there all evening giving statements, a blaady waste of time love, the cops wont do nothing about 'em."

"We were just sitting there, having a few drinks at a pub in town, aye, and there was this Maori guy. Propping up the bar, big fecka he was. Then everything just kicked off - said I looked at him funny and he didn't like it, smashed my face into the table and just left. We gave descriptions to the coppers, but they're scared of the Mongrels - won't touch 'em."

The Mongrel Mob are the largest of New Zealand's gangs, and they're mostly Maori. The Mongrels have chapters up and down the country and there are frequent outbursts of violence between rival gangs, along with some innocent by-standers in the wrong place at the wrong time. As well as the Mongrels, other gangs include Black Power, King Cobras, Head Hunters MC, Killer Beez, Greasy Dogs, Filthy Few, Satans Slaves and Dope Money Sex. The first Hells Angels chapter outside California was founded in Auckland in 1961.

With no work and few prospects, some young Maori turn to the gangs. Tempted by a lifestyle of drugs and crime, they are often drawn to the strong sense of loyalty within the gang that isn't so far removed from the Maori concept of whanau and family. Many gang members come from families that are scarred by drugs, alcohol and abuse; in fact New Zealand has one of the highest rates of domestic violence in the developed world. Besides, gang membership is increasingly lucrative as the gangs manufacture and distribute much of the country's illegal methamphetamine (meth).

Meth can induce psychosis and cerebral hemorrhage, along with being highly addictive. From a caravan's point of view, meth is a killer. Cheap and mobile, motor homes are sometimes repurposed as illegal meth labs, hidden out in the wop-wops. The poor things are filled with noxious chemicals and foul substances, before being burnt out and gutted to hide the evidence. It's a terrible way to go and no mistake.

Thankfully I've never faced such a perilous fate, though I wouldn't be surprised if Jon was toying with the idea of illegally burning the odd thing or two. We're now properly in the depths of winter, and he's trying to remain upbeat about his situation but it's tough. I'm pretty much just an oversized ice-box. Vapour clouds of steam emit from Jon in the chilled air. He sleeps in a woolly hat and socks, his clothes for the next day tucked into bed next to him, to prevent his trousers from freezing overnight. For much of the time, there is no running water, given that my pipes often freeze solid overnight. Jon has learnt to fill the kettle each night before going to bed, in order to have a much needed cup of tea in the morning.

There is a pervading smell of damp in the air. Washed t-shirts hang on clothes hangers for several days. They don't seem to dry as such, they just became slightly less wet. Jon's clothes are in danger of turning into some kind of environmental disaster, or a new strain of mould at least. A musty smell follows him around, like a poorly kept charity shop or a damp dog. In the darkness of the night, the prolonged blood curdling calls of possums taunt Jon. I interpret their calls as "I have a nice warm fur coat, what have you got?" He hasn't brushed his hair in three months and has a wild look about him, like a wild animal cornered by a vet with a hypodermic needle.

The shorter winter days have removed the benefit of the picturesque view, so it's not only the cold that presents a challenge. Our scenic surroundings have all but vanished before he returns from work - lost within the long, impenetrable darkness of night. For much of the time it's as if the world has vanished. It makes for a lonely existence.

I worry that he's depressed. His mood has darkened, and he appears less light hearted somehow. His initial unwavering love of living in the bush, and his simple existence among the stunning scenery is gone. Instead, he's weighed down with the grim slog of simply trying to keep warm and stay dry. The crisp blue sky and white gliding wisps of cloud have increasingly been replaced by grey mornings and heavy sultry clouds, inevitably laden with rain. Blue skies brought warm and breezy days while these sullen grey clouds heavily laden with rain, more often than not, brought depression. His mood seems to change with the surrounding weather and his very personality is somehow fused with the climate.

Living alone in a city is one thing, but it's quite another to live alone in the countryside. In an urban environment, you're always surrounded by street lights, the homes that surround you and the ambient sounds of traffic and your neighbours bumping about next door. You may not know them, you may not even be consciously aware of their presence but they're there. We, on the other hand, are totally isolated. I think Jon is suffering from claustrophobia, the loneliness eating away at him. He cannot wait for the weekend so he can escape me. He craves company like an insatiable hunger.

Friday 15 August

Grown adults are still scared of the dark
and for good reason. The screaming possums
may not be a genuine threat, but they sound
terrifying enough. As well as the cold, winter
brings longer nights that are much darker
than any I've experienced before. Walking
in the dark with no natural or artificial
light, I'm discovering that every sedentary
tree will gladly shove me violently into the
ground and leave me there, if I don't mind
my step.

One night in particular, I mislaid my torch
and had to navigate a short walk through the
forest as I returned to my caravan. It should
have been an inconsequential moment, but the
night sky was dense with cloud, concealing
every drop of light from the moon and
surrounding stars. My lifeline home lost, I
plunged into an abyss of absolute darkness.

I took one tentative step after another
into the forest. I waved my arms in front of
my face, but was unable to make out even a
hint of my shadow. I shut my eyes and opened
them again, realising that either way, all
I could see was the exact same image of
black nothingness. I couldn't recall ever
seeing darkness this intense before, as if
every drop of light had been sucked out of
the world. I took another step forward, and
stumbled into a tree with a crash before
pulling the pine needles out of my nose.

I'm glad I'd opted out of watching the
recent movie sensation, The Blair Witch
Project, before moving here. This is not a
place you'd want to succumb to an attack of

the heebie-jeebies. My imagination was active enough, without the thought of murderous witches and terrified film students stumbling around the caravan, screaming like a pack of wild possums. Weekends now feel like day release from prison.

"Hey!" cried out an angry voice. "What the blaady heeell d'ya theenk yeh doin'?" I'd arrived in Whangaui, and Pania had asked me to dye her hair. Sitting on a spread of old newspapers that'd been scattered over the hostel's patio, I applied the red dye, mindful not to make a mess of her or the garden furniture. Steve, the owner of the hostel, had spotted us and thrown a wobbler, reaching an eight on the Richter Scale. Shouting till he was red in the face, Steve swiftly ordered us off his property. I'd done a pretty good job though, even if I do say so myself. Although, perhaps it was fortunate that she wanted those streaks...

We headed over to Aaron's for dinner, glad to be escaping the wet and wintry weather. Aaron was a college friend of Pania's, along with being a professionally trained chef. A huge Maori fellow, Aaron had a set of shoulders like a bull and an equally gentle temperament to go with it. His home was a large white clapboard building overlooking the river. Over a dinner of melt-in-the-mouth boeuf bourguignon, Aaron told his tale of working at a ground floor restaurant at the World Trade Centre, two years previously, when it had been destroyed.

"Bro, I was lucky. I was supposed to be working in the other restaurant up on the top floor. When the first plane hit, I just got out of there as quick as I could. There was dust and glass everywhere, like a war zone…" I didn't quite know what to say. We had all seen it live on the television, but how could you ever understand what it felt like for the world to come crashing down around you? "Soon after, I left New York to visit some friends," Aaron continued. "The Feds stopped us at the airport, everyone who wasn't white was being hauled up and questioned for hours - racist bastards." Aaron's anger subsided. "Would anyone care for a muffin, fresh from the oven?" Although Aaron had retired from professional cooking, his baked muffins were still heaven sent.

New Zealand has a national obsession with muffins; their many varieties include blueberry, boysenberry, gooseberry, strawberry, chocolate, white chocolate, double chocolate, double chocolate with fudge and even spinach. I was dubious at first, when mulling over the prospect of a savoury muffin. Yet, in transforming a humble muffin into a smaller fluffier variation of a pizza, the Kiwis had invented a very tasty snack indeed. Their savoury fillings were imaginative, including the mouth watering spinach and feta cheese, ham and cheese, mushroom, and of course, the ubiquitous pumpkin. Once out of sheer desperation I'd attempted a three course meal that consisted entirely of muffins but none had tasted as delicious as these. Fresh from the oven, fluffy and warm, these muffins had a gooey jam centre that melted in the mouth like a truly exotic delicacy.

The following morning, I awoke next to Pania. Her body radiated heat, and the

sweet smell of incense sticks intermingled
with the natural scent of her body. "We've
slept in, it's nine o'clock," she whispered,
nudging me with her elbow. "Someone will see
you, you've got to leave, now!" She pulled
open the window and a rush of cold air swept
into her bedroom. "You want me to climb
out of the window?" I asked incredulously,
retrieving my clothes from her bedroom floor
and pulling them on. "My cousin might be
awake, he mustn't find out that you slept
here last night... my family, they will kill
you!" I was grateful that her bedroom was
on the ground floor as I clambered through
the window and landed on the grass outside,
pulling on a jumper in the cool morning air.
Pania gave me a gleeful smile, entertained
by my escape as she closed the window behind
me.

Until this moment, I'd thought that
climbing out of a young woman's window was
something that only happened in Hollywood
movies and romance novels. I quietly tip-
toed past her cousin's window, crept through
the garden and down the street a little way,
before turning around and returning to the
front door. "Nice morning for a walk," I
announced, walking into the kitchen, greeting
Pania with a polite "Hello". Over a bowl
of cereal, I chatted with her cousin about
cricket, having successfully concealed our
secret rendezvous.

At breakfast there was a strange sight.
His name was Lawrence and he had a broad
Glaswegian accent with a Kiwi inflection. He
was about to leave for work. The surprising
thing was that instead of a suit or a tartan

kilt, this pale white Scot was wearing full traditional Maori attire - a cloak of dried flax with a flat bladed Polynesian weapon strapped to his hip. "I'm actually half Scottish on me da's side and half Maori on me ma's, which makes me a member of the Ngati Whatau iwi," he explained before leaving.

During a less enlightened era of New Zealand's recent past, not so many years ago, the Maori were considered as extinct as the dodo. True enough, the last pure-blooded Maori had long since expired, but in recent years the definition of Maori had been extended to include anyone who could positively trace their Polynesian ancestry to one great-grandparent. Today, national statistics indicate that about one fifth of the New Zealand population claim mixed ancestry. There are a few perks too; as well as the opportunity to dress like a Polynesian warrior and scare sleepy folk over breakfast, a Maori bloodline can provide better social security benefits, as well as a subsidised university education.

We returned to a café for a leisurely Sunday. Pania succeeded in checkmating me, despite only picking up the game a few weeks ago. "I must have taught you pretty well!" I joke. She beamed with joy, laughing and teasing. "Why don't you stay another night?" she asks. It's a tempting offer, but tomorrow is Monday and I was expected at work. Reluctantly I declined. She looked at me with her best puppy-dog eyes, playfully whimpering and chuckling. We were running out of time. I was due to leave the country before long, and Pania's ex-boyfriend was

```
threatening   to   make   a   return   visit.   A
freezing cold caravan in the wop-wops seemed
like a very lonely place indeed.
```

End of diary entry

All was quiet for a week or more as Jon disappeared, travelling with friends who were visiting from overseas. When he returned it was immediately obvious that something was wrong. Apart from a weekly chat with his Mum, he rarely uses the phone so I knew something was amiss when he phones Pania.

"Hey, how you doing?" he asks, gently. "I'm ok," she answers, but she sounds tired. Jon paused. "You know, about what happened, it wasn't your fault, whatever anyone says." "It's kinda difficult to talk right now," she spoke in hushed tones. "But thanks, I appreciate it, thanks for ringing." "So you've no idea who it was?" he asks. His hand shaking as he grips the phone. "No, I don't know. I was so drunk I couldn't stand. I'm not sure, but I think he spiked my drink," she explained. "He drove me home and..."

Jon offered to visit Pania in Whanganui the next day, but she suggested that he put off his visit until the weekend after next. A final farewell, I suppose. The conversation ended. Jon put the phone down and sat still as stone. He looked pallid and drawn, as if all the blood had been drained from his body. Outside, the sky was grey, the landscape a vacuum without colour. His mood and appearance reflected the world outside, cold and washed out. Jon had become his surroundings. And as he sat, motionless, only the small vapour clouds from his mouth betrayed any sign of life and warmth.

Thursday 21 August

I stepped into the clutter of Pania's bedroom. Colourful clothes and books were strewn across the floor. A small radiator heated the room like the tropics, and a fog of incense hung heavily in the air. We stopped to drop off our bags after an afternoon's swim. Pania paused, tilting her head and for a fleeting moment she looked me in the eye. She hesitated. We seemed to read one another's thoughts, but I think we both knew that our time had been and gone. A moment's temptation soon passed.

The pair of us sat in the shared living room, as Pania carefully folded a sheet of paper into a trendy designer paper bag for a college project. The situation was complex. Her ex-boyfriend had returned and I was about to leave the country, and my time in the wop-wops was drawing to a close. I held the corners as she refolded the paper. "He's so selfish," Pania complained, "always wanting to talk about his money problems. He blames me for what happened the other night. Never shows me any affection." I really didn't know what to say. "You deserve much better than this," I replied quietly. Looking across at her, she appeared so different from the tough talking and resilient girl that I'd got to know only two months ago. She now seemed so delicate and fragile. "But you're going, Jon", she replied. "I know," I said simply. We looked at one another. "It would be different if you weren't leaving."

The following morning we breakfasted together, and then as Pania was cleaning the hostel, I went for a walk along the Whanganui River in an attempt to clear my head. I was leaving. In a week I would be moving out of the caravan. Most likely, this would be the last time I would see her. I took some small consolation in the fact that despite everything else, we remained friends.

The afternoon ticked on, and the sunlight faded. Making my excuses, I prepared to leave. Pania looked up at me with her wide doe eyes. "Don't go just yet," she implored. "Stay and dye my hair one last time, please?" I couldn't refuse. Outside, we found a grassy verge by the river next to the roadside. She sat cross-legged on the grass, with her back to me, as I worked the red dye into her short dark hair, massaging her scalp as the passing traffic slowed to see the spectacle of our al-fresco hair salon.

I couldn't put it off any longer. Throwing my backpack into the boot of the Mazda, I embraced Pania one last time and with one full turn of the steering wheel, I drove off. I couldn't resist one last glance. Pania stood, watching me leave, shrinking and disappearing in the rear-view mirror. The low sun cast long shadows across the road. I'd held on long enough, and now my chest convulsed. Wet salty tears slipped down my face. Rubbing the moisture from my eyes, I switched the indicator left, and dodged the traffic as I pulled onto Route Three. I followed the signs for the Kapiti Coast, and then I was gone.

End of diary entry

Chapter 8

Spring

Autumn may have reluctantly handed over to winter, but the change in seasons to spring is vital and sudden. Almost overnight, dark clouds vanish and light pours in through my windows like I am being reborn. The sun shines with invigorated warmth, dissolving the frosted dew that drips from my roof, as the world quickly defrosts. Each evening the sun is in less of a hurry to depart, and the days become progressively longer. The taller forested peaks, once capped with snow, finally return to their natural colour. Even the birds return. The tui who we haven't heard for many months came back with a joyful click, whirr and whistle.

Jon was preparing to leave. The long winter has left me with a thick deposit of twigs and dead grass over my floor, and I resemble some kind of massive nest. My windows and doors have been sealed shut to maintain a semblance of warmth, but now they are thrown open to blow away the damp, dusky air. My furniture lifted outside to sit on the grass, as Jon sweeps my floors and wipes down my shelves. Mildew scented clothes hang on a washing line. Not everything survived the onslaught of the seasons. His straw hat has developed a fatal case of mould, and is a gonner for sure.

There are no long farewells. The following morning, he locks my door one last time and leaves this wild place of birds and forest, silence and seasons and rejoins the modern world.

Thursday 28 August

I confess that it was with some relief that
I was returning to the relative luxuries of
central heating, hot running water and dry
clothes to wear. But despite the appalling
cold of the winter and the solitude of the
place, I'd learnt to love my little caravan.
Not least, the simple pleasure of looking
out over the dying sunlight as it refracted
over the forested hills. I'd miss the way my
home shifted and creaked in the wind, and the
sight of the endless star-filled night skies.

Life in the bush could be hard, even with
a car and a supermarket close by. The utter
absence of warmth, and having to crawl under
the electric blanket to eat my dinner each
night had made life almost unbearable at
times. There are many stories of isolationists
living in their huts in solitude, apart from
society and quite happy with their lot. But
they all had one advantage that I lacked:
an open fire and a reliable source of heat.
Wearing socks in bed just didn't cut it.

Nevertheless this place, this lone caravan
had burnt an indelible impression upon me.
I couldn't say for certain how, but the
experience had definitely changed me. Living
in the wop-wops, I had discovered that life
became simpler, and the world seemed like
a less complicated place. By abandoning
so many things and learning to live with
fewer distractions, I found that nervous,
restless tension can be left behind, only
to be replaced with a deep sense of peace
and calm. I felt emboldened, yet humbled by
living so close to the elements. I was aware

of a clarity of mind and a sense of removal from myself, and a stillness that can be found from retreat.

To truly experience this wild, untamed place is a stark reminder that nature is vast and unforgiving. A soundtrack of strange bumps and creaks of the trees, howls and screams of the possums raging against the southerly gales, that can play with you and toss you about for amusement. Humans are not the centre of the world, though it's not easy to see that when you're in a city among thousands of people.

I've come to the conclusion that to travel the world means nothing, if you don't allow the experience to change you. With the age of exploration long since dead and buried, every continent, every island, every corner of every forest tagged, mapped and catalogued, the only journey worth the trouble is to explore your own mind. If travelling doesn't change the way you think, then you haven't really travelled.

End of diary entry

I've noticed how the wop-wops have changed Jon, these last few months. He's not the only one though. The remoteness of New Zealand has profoundly affected every living soul in the country. Our distinct land-dwelling birdlife would never have evolved the way they had, if New Zealand had been within floating distance of mammals. And when humankind finally made an appearance and introduced mammals to New Zealand, the relative safety of this country's remote corners, its wop-wops and outlying islands ensured the survival of these unique creatures. There have been some casualties along the way, but many species continue to survive, although only the takahe has officially been brought back from the dead.

Despite doom-laden predictions of the end of the Maori, their way of life has also firmly endured, partly thanks to the great distance the Europeans had to travel to reach New Zealand. The remoteness slowed down colonisation, preventing a sudden and massive influx, and buying the Maori enough time to adapt and survive. This same distance also gave the Maori a separate sense of identity, quite distinct from that of the Polynesian islands they'd left behind. And despite the contemporary social problems, a promising future lies ahead for New Zealand's Polynesian descendants. The success story of Kaikoura, a resurgence of interest in Maori culture and the belated retributions for the broken promises from the Treaty of Waitangi are just a few indicators of this positive change.

As for Kiwi identity, those hardy pioneers who left the Old World and found themselves living out in the bush are definitely not forgotten. The local shop may no longer be a week's hike away, but those resourceful qualities prevail to this day. Many a Kiwi bloke can be found tinkering in his shed or garage, building something out of nothing, with invention now a recreational past-time. The modern Kiwi continues to explore new ways to part tourists from their money, by finding yet another original way of throwing people from mountains. Adapt and survive, that's evolution for you.

And finally, turning to the place of a lone wild caravan in today's New Zealand, to many I am simply a one man shanty town. I might represent an abandoned holiday home or a national embarrassment, a lingering reminder of the continuing poverty in this country. Contrary to what the tourist posters suggest, most New Zealanders have chosen an urban lifestyle and do not live in the wop-wops. But as the historian Michael King noted, New Zealanders still cling to the 'man alone' tradition, even when they're many miles from the bush. You might find books, photos, even exhibitions dedicated to me, the New Zealand wild caravan. I have my fans and loyal followers, and the lucky few who stay with me can find out what it means to live on the outer edge of the modern world. In these quiet places amid the rustle of the forest, you might just hear the rhythm of your own heart.

A Note from the Author

I hope you enjoyed reading Squashed Possums as much as I enjoyed writing it – which would not have been possible without the help of my trusty caravan. Can I please invite you to leave a short review on Amazon or Goodreads? As a new novelist, just a few lines would mean a great deal to me and my former home.

Check out my website for more information and why not read some more travel stories? Or you can get in touch with me at:

Web: www.jontindale.com
Twitter: @jontindale
Email: tindalejon@gmail.com

About the Author

Jonathan Tindale is five foot, eleven and a half inches tall and consists mostly of unruly hair. Many years after leaving New Zealand, he still dresses like he lives in the wop-wops despite working in Westminster, because, in his words, he 'works in digital'. He can often be found in National Trust houses with his wife Amy and son, William, where his friendly banter with the volunteers is often misconstrued as making untoward advances. He is almost 40 years old but he is ok with that (mostly).

Bibliography

The Caravan, Pataka Museum of Arts & Cultures, Porirua

Vantastic: A Pictorial History of Caravans in New Zealand by Chris Hunter Publisher is: Flamingo

Outsiders - Stories from the fringe of New Zealand society by Gerard Hindmarsh- Craig Potton Publishing

The Penguin History of New Zealand by Michael King Penguin Books

A Man's Country?: The image of the Pakeha Male by Jock Phillips Penguin Books

Walden: Life in the Woods by Henry David Thoreau Ticknor and Fields, Boston

Exclusive Material

Reading group discussion questions

Deleted scenes

Skydiving: the wop-wops from 15,000 feet

Additional short stories

1. Tokyo: Santa with chopsticks
2. Big Gay Aleppo
3. The great Beijing tea heist
4. Macau: dirty money
5. Ecuador: how not to exfoliate your face on a volcano
6. Ecuador: an ice cream revolution
7. Beirut: a nasty run in with a taxi driver
8. Dating in Damascus

Reading group discussion questions

1. If the lone caravan represents New Zealand because it is isolated - what other objects would you choose to represent other countries?

2. How would you have reacted and behaved if you found yourself in Jon's place, living in a lonely caravan in New Zealand?

3. If the character of the lone caravan is a work of fiction but the events that took place really happened, is this a work of fiction or non-fiction? Discuss.

4. Have you ever lived in a house that feels like it gets to know the occupants? What would your home say about you?

Skydiving: the wop-wops from 15,000 feet

I t's a perfect day today for a sky-jump. You sure you want to book for tomorrow?" Having met up with friends, we were standing in the hostel reception desk arranging a sky-jump for the following day. A quick online weather check revealed that tomorrow might be a washout. The woman behind the desk ran through to check, "Yeah, how about in a couple hours? Sure thing." We'd opted for the 15,000 feet jump, the highest altitude possible without the use of oxygen masks. Well, might as well go the whole hog, I reasoned. A flock of butterflies performed acrobatics in my stomach. At least there wasn't time to fret about it. "Most fun you can have with your clothes on" I'd been promised. I wasn't convinced, but I'd be willing to give it a try. Get on a plane, take off, and simply jump out - how hard could it be?

Arriving at the airstrip and waiting patiently for our turn, we watched the colourful parachutes faintly appear in the sky, one by one, twisting in the air and floating to the ground. I was a little nervous, but this display made it seem manageable. I reckoned I could handle this. A few feet away, a van was serving up burgers. How anyone could contemplate eating fast food, or any food, before jumping out of a plane is beyond me. My bladder was beginning to feel the pressure, and I went to use the toilet. There was one single small window overlooking the opposite side of the skydiving centre with worryingly thick steel bars across the window-frame. I guess that the extra level of security is to prevent anyone from making a break for it, thanks to last-minute nerves. I can't say that I wasn't tempted.

A short instructional video, accompanied to a pounding techno soundtrack to supposedly build our excitement and adrenaline, explained that we'd be fastened to a professional diving partner. This total stranger would have done hundreds if not thousands of dives, but my first encounter with them would involve lots of spooning and strapping, before our big mutual jump. The video then showed the spooner and spoonee falling to the ground with all the aerodynamic ability of a wet bag of concrete for a full minute, before the parachute opened and allowed it's wearers to float gently to the ground.

Pulling on our jump-suits, gloves, Biggles style goggles and crash helmets, we were introduced to our tandem diving partners. Mine seemed like a decent bloke, not very chatty, but most importantly he didn't seem depressed. A light airplane landed nearby, skipping quickly across the short airstrip. We clambered aboard, sitting on the floor, our jump partners behind us. Accelerating along the airstrip, we left the safety of the ground behind. As the plane rose, the view through the shaking clear plastic slide door became increasingly distant. At five thousand feet the sky-dive centre looked like a toytown. This was the altitude that our 'chute would open. Climbing further, at 10,000 feet the temperature began to drop dramatically, clouds of carbon dioxide gasped from our mouths as we smiled nervously at one another.

Lake Taupo, below us, looked barely larger than a puddle - despite the lake being only slightly smaller than the whole of Singapore. Until this moment, I had been remarkably composed, and happy to enjoy the view while my brain was in utter denial of what was about to happen. Jump out of a plane? Don't be silly! I was closest to the door and would be the first to jump, as we gave one another a final, tentative thumbs-up. My jump partner attached the clips, fastening us together and all of a sudden, without any final questions or comments, the slide door was flung open. Creeping towards the howling, terrifying gale blowing into the already freezing un-pressurised plane, I feigned a smile at the digital camera, as the blood drained from my face, aghast at the dawning realisation of what I was about to do.

"Aaaaaaaaaaaaaaaaaaaaaagh!"

The first thing I noticed, as my body accelerated towards the ground, was a glimpse of the plane disappearing in the distance. Tumbling and somersaulting through the air, I briefly spotted the small plane before it very quickly vanished from view. Releasing my arms from the harness, I felt the air currents crashing violently against me.

Disorientated and freezing cold, my mind was still in some state of shock, as it concentrated upon holding my terrified sanity together. Despite falling at a terrific speed, at such a height, my mind didn't seem to register that I was falling to the ground. Instead I seemed to be falling in every direction, and to make matters worse motion sickness violently kicked in. The constant tumbling, spinning and somersaulting were taking their toll, as I was thrown around in the air with no control over my mad movements. By the time we'd reached five thousand feet, we had been plummeting towards the earth for an entire minute. My face was rippling in the air currents, as we reached speeds of two hundred kilometres per hour.

Somewhere in the deafening roar, I heard a shout, and I looked back to see my partner signalling that I grip hold of the harness. The 'chute suddenly shot open, with the sound of rattling canvas and as if a giant hand had plucked us from the air, and with that the winds ceased and instead we began to float. I attempted a loud 'WOOHOO" but it came out more like a feeble and relieved "wooo". I felt like my entire body had undergone the single most traumatising event in its twenty-eight year history, and everything had turned to jelly. My mind still hadn't come to terms with whatever on earth, and not on the earth, was happening to me. Breathe. Just a few more seconds, I thought, and it'll all be over.

"YOU ALRIGHT, MAAAEEETE???" my diving buddy hollered, as he threw the parachute into a series of dramatic tailspins, and impressive but violent twists and turns. I gave it to him straight: "IF YOU DON'T STOP DOING THAT, I'M GOING TO BE SICK ON YOU!!!"

Thankfully my overenthusiastic diving partner wisely calmed the motion of our descent, and for the first time since falling out of the plane I felt something close to enjoyment as we gently floated and descended. More than anything though, I was relieved to have survived the ordeal, having spotted the sky-dive centre reassuringly close beneath us. Within a few short seconds, I was lifting up my feet and landing softly in a large pile of shingle. I ran my gloved hands through the little stones, in sweet appreciation of a safe landing and the joy of being back on planet earth, I even kissed the ground.

August 2003

Tokyo: Santa
with chopsticks

After a long day trekking the streets of Tokyo, I returned to my budget ryokan in the downtown district of Minowa. With a final few hours in Japan, I was all set for a quiet evening of packing. I sat sipping a cup of green tea, my nose in a book, when a Mongolian looking man strode into the lounge. "We need Father Christmas, will you be Father Christmas?" I blinked, a little stunned, "What, now?" I asked. "Yes, yes, Father Christmas. We have costume, give you free Japanese meal, must come now!" he explained with a sense of grave urgency.

Well, how could I refuse - it was almost Christmas after all. He walked me down a dark road to another local hotel, where a woman welcomed us in. Little was said except for "Thank you, thank you, thank you".With a little help, I donned the familiar red jacket and trousers, hat and white beard. But I looked too skinny to be Santa, so we stuffed a cushion into my jacket, tied into place with an obi. I necked a cup of sake, which fortunately, was as strong as paint stripper. I was then led down the backstreets of downtown Tokyo, dressed like Santa, with a big sack of presents for the kids. I wasn't expecting to be abandoned outside a small Japanese restaurant, left with only the sage advice "Merry Christmas!"

Alone, I took a deep breath and slid open the door. Stepping into the bright light of the restaurant, I almost felt like I was stepping onto a stage. For a moment, time seemed to stop. More than a dozen little faces looked up at me, and the children's mothers faced me expectantly. The guys behind the bar peered around, beers in hand, I delivered an almighty "Merry Christmas Everyone!!" and threw in a few "Ho-ho-hos" for good measure. The whole place erupted with cheers and applause. The children queued patiently and politely for their presents, which turned out to be a selection of Hello Kitty Easter eggs. I was sat at the mothers' table, very few of whom spoke a word of English. Plates of sashimi, oyster tempura, and rice cakes were placed before me, as I tried to explain that my stomach was an artificial one. Although everything was very "oshi" - delicious, I said that I couldn't possibly manage it all.

A little girl approached me with a pencil and notepaper, and I was told that she wanted the autograph of Father Christmas. As I obliged, the other utterly star-struck children waited in line for their own dedications. Their mobile 'handy' phones were held aloft, posing for photographs with Santa. I later found out that the restaurant manager had been looking several days for a gaijin - foreigner - to dress up as Santa. She'd been standing outside the local subway station in the cold, trying to find a suitable and willing volunteer. I was introduced to the family, her husband who repeatedly said "thank you, thank you" and a wizened old mother who was the head sushi chef. I attempted polite conversation with the mums. They giggled nervously behind their hands. "Where you from?", "Japan - vacation or business?", "You single?"

A Christmas cake was soon brought out, laden with candles. Everyone was trying to tell me something, but I couldn't tell what it was. Did they want to me to cut the cake? Hand out the slices? I was then given a pair of chopsticks, and taken to the children's table. With a few more "Ho-ho-hos" to their eager faces, the cake was presented and the candles were lit. A dozen children blew them out, before unsnapping their chopsticks and piling into the cream cake in an unrestrained feeding frenzy. I grabbed my own chopsticks and joined in, plucking at the strawberries and creamy cake, and shoveling it down like a good big-bellied Santa should.

Finally, the mothers instructed their children to sing a Japanese song. The moment was very kusai - cute, that is, until the song finished, and everyone asked me to sing. Oh gawd, a Karaoke Christmas! My mind went utterly blank. Jingle Bells? Forgotten it. Rudolph the Red Nose Reindeer? Forgot that too. Then, with a smile I remembered, "We wish you a Merry Christmas and a Happy New Year, Good tidings we bring to you and your King..." I stumbled through a rendition, reaching the end of the song with a tidal wave of relief. Again, the restaurant whooped and applauded.

I was Father Christmas, albeit a fake fat Santa with chopsticks!

December 2003

Big Gay Aleppo

In Syria, people are often not what they seem. For starters, there are a surprising number of Arabic George Bush fans, who cheer him on for flattening neighbouring Iraq whilst bankrupting the American economy.

Every American I've met is pretending to be Canadian. There are quite a few Americans kicking about in Syria, despite the rather severe warnings on the CIA travel website. Most of them are studying Arabic at the University of Cairo and travelling through the Middle East during their term breaks. They're drawn here to practice their new language skills and experience the places they've been reading about.

"So, what sort of job do you think you'll end up doing?" I asked one, curious at how their passports would be handled by US Customs. "Most graduates go into government," he answered. "Some end up as teachers, a few journalists, secret services, that sort of thing." I suppose pretending to be Canadian was good practice for international diplomacy. "And that works, does it?" I enquired. "Sure, it works", he answered. "Well, it works until someone asks me what the capital of Canada is, I never could remember..." The Arabs aren't stupid. Most know full well that there can't be that many Canadians in the Middle East, but take it in good humour. More worryingly, the American secret intelligence is set to be populated by people who don't know what the capital of Canada is.

And it's not just the Americans. One guy I met was dating a Lebanese Druze - a secretive offshoot of Shiite Islam whose population largely reside in the mountains of Lebanon. Conversion to or from the faith is strictly prohibited, as is presumably, fooling around with an American who thinks he might be Canadian. Should any locals enquire in a friendly sort of way where she was from, she'd claim that she was French. Unfortunately this tactic had its own set of problems; since being an ex-French colony, a lot of Syrians either speak French or have a better knowledge of France's geography than most Brits. The lady in question, however, had never even set foot in Europe. They made quite the couple, an American pretending to be Canadian and a Lebanese who was claiming to be French. But even this pair's confused identity had nothing on the locals in Aleppo, who busy themselves with pretending to be homosexual.

Aleppo competes with Damascus for the title of the world's oldest continually inhabited city, and it shows. Aleppo's souk is a fascinating hodgepodge of shopping and history. Imagine a department store that had moved into a museum, with the souk housed in an ancient stone tunnel. Intricately carved, its stores stand between hammam baths and prayer halls. Through the magnificent but gnarled stone gate of Bab Antakya, each stall competes for the customer's attention with a friendly sales patter of "Very good price, just for you!" and offers of hot sweet tea. My eye was caught by a pile of brightly coloured table cloths and scarves. "Peshwaan. Very good price", I was told by a persistent young Arab. "Where you from?" he asked and without pausing for an answer, continued "I study in Cambridge, very expensive, you want tea?" His conversation was relentless. I was being asked if I wanted tea in a sort of question, but to turn him down would have clearly been a gross insult. I tried to explain that he'd have better luck extracting blood from a stone than persuading me to buy a tablecloth, but he insisted. "No buy, just talk." I sat on a stack of rugs, sipping a glass of hot sweet tea. He appeared to be wearing make-up.

His plump business partner emerged from the back of the stall. "Hello young maaan!" he announced in a high pitched voice, waving his arms with an overly dramatic flourish. I'd somehow stumbled into the Syrian equivalent of the Pink Palace. This guy was so camp that he made the most flamboyant of male flight attendants look straight. Surveying each customer passing his stall, he threw up his arms in dismay. "Darling! There are just too many Turks today," he spat. "It's not good business, all quantity, no quality!" He went on to explain that with the celebration of Eid, the final day of Ramadan, neighbouring Syria and Turkey opened their border without charge. The result is a sudden influx of Turks into Aleppo. "Surely that's good for business?" I asked. "But they have no money, waste of time," he muttered. Clearly frustrated with the standard of his customers, he sighed. I swiftly made a diplomatic exit, continuing along the market.

I headed towards the medieval Citadel and had almost escaped the souk, when I fell in step with a chap who had noticed my guidebook. He introduced himself. "My name is Sebastian, I am in your book - look!" He plucked the Lonely Planet from my hand, flicking through the pages. "I have a shop. You are invited, please come in. Not to buy, to practice English please. I had exam in only two weeks." It had been at least ten minutes since my last cup of tea, and it was pretty clear that he was about to fail on his tenses, so I accepted his offer. Like everyone else in the souk, he was wearing rouge, eye-liner and half his mother's make-up box.

"So, are you visiting Syria with your wife?" he enquired with a camp inflection. "No", I answered. "Girlfriend?" he asked. "No", I answered. "Are you with a boyfriend?" he teased. "No, no!" I insisted, "I'm just travelling by myself." Behind Sebastian, amongst the shelves of jewellery, hubbly-bubbly pipes and colourful embroideries was a weathered poster of Oscar Wilde, complete with Dorian Gray quotations. The display seemed quite appropriate really. After all, Wilde led a double life and Dorian Gray spent his life pretending to be someone he wasn't. In the Aleppo souk, Sebastian explained that homosexuality is just a gimmick. The salesmen pretend to be gay to snag the curiosity of surprised tourists, and exploit their confusion to sell them something. Then they all go home to their wives and families. As for the seemingly effeminate Sebastian, he was engaged to be married in just a few weeks time. His wife-to-be is probably a Sunni Muslim pretending to be from Ottowa.

November 2004

The great Beijing tea heist

After a long day of exploring, I wanted nothing more than a quiet cup of tea. And that's how I found myself sitting in a traditional tea house in downtown Beijing. The door was shut. I was surrounded, having been presented with a jaw dropping bill of more than a thousand yen, around £100. I wouldn't mind if it was a ten course silver service affair, but I'd only had a couple cups of tea and some nibbles. I'd been scammed, hook, line and sinker. I was as angry with myself, as I was with the conspirators around me. Duped and done over, all for the sake of a pot of tea.

According to legend, the habit of drinking tea developed in China almost 5,000 years ago. The emperor Shennong preferred his drinking water to be boiled. One day, a dead leaf from a wild tea bush flew into his boiled water. The servant gave the drink to his emperor. Luckily for the servant, the emperor was more refreshed than furious and cha (tea) was invented. The importance of tea cannot be underestimated in China. Monks used tea to convey peace and humility. In the eighth century, Lu Yu's "The Classic Art of Tea' was published. Consequently the making of tea was elevated to an art form which ushered in tea ceremonies, still popular across China and Japan to this day. Tea is also used for medicinal purposes, from aiding digestion to playing a part in complex and expensive remedies that can be purchased from the local herbalist.

It was a cold winter's day as I walked across Tiananmen Square. I hadn't spoken more than a few words of English since I'd arrived in Beijing, some three days ago. A Chinese girl approached me, closely followed by two friends. "Where you from?" they asked. I explained that I was from London. They were students from Tsingtao, the city where the beer comes from. One mentioned that she was studying to be a teacher, and wanted to practice her English. I was happy to have a conversation, and reluctant to pass up the opportunity to talk to a local. As I carefully shifted my backpack to my chest, I thought I was smart to the various tricks and misdirections that are often used by thieves.

We were all headed to the Forbidden Palace, but they rightly pointed out that it was too late to visit that day. So we decided to walk around the old neighbourhoods instead. We talked about how expensive city life is, and how Beijingers often don't understand their regional dialect. We fussed about the weather, and someone suggested that we go for tea to thaw out. It was a reasonable suggestion, and one that I'd welcomed. After all, we'd been walking and talking for some two or three hours and the temperature hadn't risen much above freezing since I'd first arrived in Beijing.

We walked through a tea house and into a private room around the back, which looked strangely panda friendly with mock bamboo walls. The table was laid out with a few snacks, and the pots of tea soon arrived. We're served green tea and oolong, and drink from small decorative cups. My new friend asks if there are many Chinese in London and I reply that yes, "I am married to one of them", and show them a picture of my wife, Amy. "Woah!" they exclaim, surprised. The conversation continues to roll along amiably. I was relaxed, my initial suspicions long since subsided. And then the bill arrived.

I looked down at the scrap of paper and up again. Everyone is watching me expectantly. I felt my blood running cold as if a draught had blown through the room. "There must be some mistake", I protested. And they repeatedly responded: "No, no". I pointed to the prices on the wall, behind me. "But it says there, 20 or 30 yen for a cup of tea." "Ah, but those prices are for cups of tea, not the pots of tea that we'd ordered" The proprietor moves a plant and the rest of the menu, previously concealed, is revealed: 380 yen for a pot of tea. Oh, that is crafty.

My new friends scraped their money together. "You don't have to pay everything" they explained, "Just your share". I knew I'd been had, but having just spent the past three hours talking to these people, I still couldn't quite believe they were in on it. I figured I'd had maybe half a dozen cups of tea, a few crisps and a bit of fruit. I put down 200 yen to cover my share of the bill. "Oh, we don't have enough", they observed. So I put down another 100 note which brought my total to around £30. I firmly explained that this was the limit, and I wasn't going to pay anymore. I got up to leave, despite a still awkward atmosphere because we hadn't yet covered the bill. One of them got up with me, to help find an ATM. I quickly said goodbye, grabbed my bag and headed out the door. I returned to my hotel, angry and shaken. And sadly, my fears were confirmed. A quick search on Google was all that was needed to reveal that the tea heist is a notorious scam in Beijing. I could have kicked myself, but the deception had been professionally executed. They had earned my trust first, concealing their intent beneath a deceitful yet plausible friendship. I consulted my travel companion, a collection of sayings by Confucius, who offered some sympathy. "It is easy to evade the lance but not the hidden sword."

November 2009

Macau:
dirty money

Next to my feet is a bucket of water, half full of loose change – not exactly what I expect to find in the historic A-ma temple of Macau. We follow the winding path through the temple and take in the scenery, noticing the boulders that sit atop the surrounding hillside. Each is inscribed with sage advice on enlightenment and modesty, which seems horribly ironic. If the temple preaches modesty, then why is there a minimum donation of 10 Hong Kong dollars? But this doesn't seem to dampen anyone's enthusiasm, as another coin hits the water with a thirsty splash.

An ex-Portuguese colony, Macau was handed back to China shortly after the British returned neighbouring Hong Kong. Until recently, Macau was a backwater, albeit a picturesque one with a strong European influence. The ruined gothic façade of the church of St Paul stands dramatically amongst the black and white tiles. Along the cobbled streets there is a pervasive smell of fresh custard tarts, and salesmen are eager to offer you a sample of the local sweet sticky pork.

With the sun on our faces and a delicious plate of Portuguese bacalhau (creamy fish and potatoes) in front of us, we wash it all down with sangria. We might have been in Lisbon, but the illusion is soon punctured, by stalls of Maoist nick-nacks and oil paintings depicting the triumph of the Red Army. This is China after all, and yet Mao seems even further away than the European missionaries who arrived all those centuries ago.

Macau might still have a Portuguese flavour, but today there is a stronger influence at work - Las Vegas, Macau remains the only place you can gamble in a casino in China and after the handover, high rise casinos popped up like mushrooms all over the islands. In 2006, the upstart Macau overtook the more experienced Vegas, earning $6.8billion in casino revenue compared to Las Vegas' $6.6 billion.

Don't feel too sorry for the Americans though. After all, US investors own many of these new competitor casinos in Macau. The latest addition to the flickering neon skyline is the Venetian, a colossal 3,000 room labyrinth of a hotel, with black jack tables and high-stakes baccarat. I quickly lost ten quid on the roulette wheel, before discovering that watching our surroundings is more entertaining and considerably less costly.

Chinese mainlanders crowd around the tables and seriously concentrate on their game, pausing only to swear occasionally in Mandarin. Young working girls in skimpy dresses work the tables in hungry packs, hunting for the big winners who are likely to exchange hard currency for a good time. Everyone avoids eye contact with the man with a scarred face and gnarled thumb, who angrily thumps his broken fist down on the table.

The hotel owners understand that there is more than one way to part the public from their money. An artificial Venetian lagoon has been created, like the one in Vegas, complete with gondola rides and a cloudless blue sky. Chinese tourists escape from the tables to take a consolation ride on a gondola, or spread their new found wealth across the high-end boutique and lavish ching-bling jewellery emporiums. A Chinese duplication of a Las Vegas copy of a European city may seem unnecessary, but you can be sure the hotel's investors are laughing all the way to the Hang Seng bank.

There is a great deal of money pouring into Macau, but not all of it is clean. The vast majority of cash pours in from the mainland, and a large chunk of that is from the black economy. Every new construction project in China, and there are many, faces an array of kickbacks and bribes which filter through the relevant officials and contractors. A lot of the cash ends up on the tables in Macau. Behind closed doors, the real money is gambled in private rooms where the stakes can be astronomically high. It's fun though, walking through the casino, never sure if the suitcase rolling by is filled with dirty laundry or dirty money.

In Vegas, you can take a tourist bus to learn how the wise-guys once ruled the city. But in Macau, they still do. During our stay, the news focussed on the arrest of Macau's former Minister of Transport. He was charged with 76 criminal offences, from bribery and money laundering to abuse of power. More recent protests have set their sights on Macau's leader himself, the Chief Executive Edmund Ho.

Meanwhile back at the A-ma temple, a coup had taken place. The local residents had accused the old monk of corruption, so he was being physically removed from his temple. As we left, he continued to protest his innocence, particularly to the surrounding film crews and journalists.

Yet on the floor, buckets of water continue to fill up with Macau's dirty money...

November 2007

Ecuador: how not to exfoliate your face on a volcano

Do you want to get away from the tired tourist sites? Maybe get a different perspective on a place? Then why not experience a country's health service, by impressively smashing yourself up in a terrible accident? No - don't fancy it? I didn't think so. But having done just this, I thought I'd share my experience, so others can reap the rewards.

Crashing and somersaulting head first over the handlebars of a quad bike isn't the smartest thing I've ever done. But then, hurtling face first into a gravel track and running myself over didn't exactly improve matters. As I sped round the corner, I had seen the ridge in the middle of the road coming towards me, but there was nowhere near enough time to brake. In one confusing and completely disorientating moment, I was tangled among the fast moving machinery, as the bike performed a grotesque dance around me. I blacked out. When I came to, the bike had dragged me 30 feet down the road before coming to an abrupt halt, upside down in a ditch.

I tried to get up, but my legs were like blancmange and I quickly collapsed. I was hurt - my left hand lacerated with deep bloody scratches. My face was bloody and raw. Trust me, never exfoliate your face at high speed on a gravel track, especially while freewheeling down a volcano on a quad bike. It's messy, painful and really quite unhygienic.

I sat there in shock, as a pair of Ecuadorian octogenarians interrupted their afternoon stroll with a concerned "com estas?" I couldn't remember enough Spanish to give an honest answer, so instead I improvised with an unconvincing "Estoy bien."

Before long I was back at the hostel, cleaning my wounds. To my relief, a rush of endorphins swamped my system as I plucked the gravel and dead flesh from the gaping wound below my knee. My leg looked like it had been attacked by a lunatic who was armed with a sharp ice cream scoop. My friend, Jorik, treated my wounds. The pain was excruciating, and the room must have looked like a torture scene. Playing the role of the mad doctor, he politely asked to spray my open wounds with medicinal alcohol. The pain was beyond words and we collapsed into hysterical laughter.

The following day passed with little to distinguish it from any other. But what I didn't immediately do was visit a doctor. Why? It's hard to say. Was it the good old stiff upper lip? A little. Was I in denial over the state of my injuries? Perhaps. Was it a fear of Ecuador's medicinal services? Absolutely.

What happened later that afternoon might be attributed to fate, God, or a guardian angel. I don't draw such links, though perhaps I should. "Can I interest you boys in some nice fresh coffee? Not Nescafe," she insisted. The woman had a thick German accent. A big lady, she looked like she'd served some hard time in a bakery. "Hey, what happened to your face?" she enquired. With heavy bandaging and a precarious limp, my injuries were all too apparent. I explained what had happened. "They're bloody dangerous those things," she explained, rather unnecessarily. "A kid the other day, he tried to run a police road block. Crashed his quad bike and took his head clean off." Gulp. She wasn't impressed that I hadn't seen a doctor. "You're too young to lose your looks and you don't want scars. There's a clinic just down the next road - you should go..."

What was I thinking? I must have been out of my mind not to see a doctor. I thanked her and before I knew it, I was expressed past the queue at the local clinic and promptly ordered to lay flat out on a coach. My doctor was Russian and didn't speak a word of English. We skipped Spanish and instead communicated in broken German via my Dutch friend, Jorik. "He says your wounds are infected and you need, uh, what is the word?" I get the gist, as the doctor stabs another anti-inflammatory into my infected face. "Ouch!" I stared at the ceiling and tried not to watch. I was utterly helpless as the doctor quietly stitched my wounds with a thick black thread, more like bootlace than something you'd expect to find an operating room. I'd been Frankensteined.

With some relief, we returned to the Secret Garden in Quito. The family run hostel was to become a home from home during my convalescence. In such a short time, these strangers, my hosts and fellow travellers had donated medication, offered advice, sympathy and a steady pair of hands to cleanse my wounds. I don't know what I would have done without them, and was rather touched when Maya nicknamed me the 'The English Patient'. Hang on though, didn't he die?

April 2006

Ecuador: an ice cream revolution

Ecuador announced a state of emergency, just a few days before I arrived in the capital of Quito. "Oh don't worry about that," said the Peruvian journalist, as he sat next to me on the plane and tried to reassure me. His name was Ernesto, and shared his name with Ernesto 'Che' Guevara. "This happens all the time in South America." He went on to explain his upbringing during the 1980's, the hey-day of the Shining Path guerrillas. "Street curfews, blockades," he shrugged, "these were everyday news." If the country was collapsing into a state of anarchy, then at least it wasn't anything new.

These particular protests were over the free trade agreement, an initiative to remove barriers to trade between the USA and along with several other countries, Ecuador. Interim President Palacio had recommended the agreement to his people, as had George Bush to the US Congress. I hadn't heard whether senators and congressmen were blockading Washington with burning tyres for several days, but this was certainly the response in Ecuador.

I hadn't been in the country more than an hour or two. Just enough time to get a cab to a friendly backpacker's hotel in the historic old town of Quito. The view from the hostel balcony was stunning. In the distance, the city streets tumble down the steep Andean mountainside like an avalanche of colonial masonry. Among the church towers and monasteries stood the Virgin of Quito, with a watchful eye over the city from her hill-top vantage point.

I was busily and happily soaking up my surroundings, when a long haired Kiwi in dreadlocks approached me. "Mate, there's a protest just down the road. You should get down there and take your camera, the army are firing tear gas in every direction - you could get some great photos!"

The Swedish couple nearby politely declined, but I cautiously stepped out from the refuge of the hostel, still wobbly with jet lag. Taking my first steps into the city, I noticed the street was cobbled, its buildings tightly terraced with one in particular featuring a small barbers' selling grotesque carnival masks. Turning the corner, I was almost knocked clean off my feet. A surging crowd swept past me. They were all wearing the traditional brightly coloured ponchos of the Andes, with pork-pie bowler hats perched upon their heads and hankies stretched across their faces. In close pursuit were half the Ecuadorian army, identifiable in their urban grey camouflage. Well, mostly grey. For some inexplicable reason, a few wore pinkish purple uniforms that gave them the appearance of Amsterdam's 1st Battalion Rainbow Division.

The air was already thin due to the altitude, and didn't do much to dilute a lungful of tear gas. It tasted peppery and slightly abrasive but within moments, it had cleared up my sinuses a treat. A taste of the protests had brought much of the country to its knees. Even the price of food had gone up in the city, because nothing could get through from the outlying farming areas. Travelling was virtually impossible. One young family from British Colombia explained how they had returned to Quito, by managing to persuade a local guide to take them over a remote pass by horseback to avoid the roads. At least it had provided their two young daughters with an adventurous holiday tale, which surely must rival the imagination of their classmates. During my own travels, I found myself hauled off a bus by uniformed men toting automatic weapons, and told to press my hands against the side of the vehicle.

So what did the locals make of it all? Almost everyone I spoke to was in sympathy with the protestors. Hailing down a taxi, the driver negotiated a situation on the road with a casual "No problemo" before winding up the windows and hitting the gas. He, like many others, summed up the general mood of the country. Ecuador was just not ready to compete with the cheap imports of the USA's super sized and subsidised farming industry.

But the fifty million dollar question is this: will a trade agreement with the gringos leave Ecuador better or worse off. The US administration's continuing subsidies of their own agricultural exports are a major point of contention, and make a mockery of free trade. But this isn't really about economics anymore. Many Ecuadorians are suspicious of their own government's motives, but most have nothing but outright contempt for the gringo US administration. All over South America there is a massive anti-USA backlash taking place, in particular with President Chavez in Venezuela, and the Bolivian government nationalising their energy industry. If you thought ol' Dubya was unpopular in Britain, it pales in comparison to the quantity of 'F**K Bush' graffiti you see around the streets of Quito.

Sadly, the option to simply refuse to sign up isn't a particularly viable one, either. If Ecuador doesn't sign the agreement, then danger lies ahead. The harsh reality is that they'll lose all their US trade to neighbouring rivals Colombia or Peru, or whoever else is prepared to sign on the dotted line. A lose-lose situation, pretty much. But there's always a bright side. There is one group of people who are making a few extra bucks at the moment. Situated at every road blockade, among the groups of local protestors and the armed police, is a little stripy wagon that's being pushed along.

He is the ice-cream salesmen, and with his catchphrase "Saledo, saledo!' he shifts thousands of frosted ices to both sides. These guys are doing such good business, that it's rare to see a policeman or soldier without an ice-cream stuck in his gob. At least the army are temporarily distracted from tear gassing and hitting people with their truncheons for a few moments.

It's just as well I'm not of a suspicious mind, or I might suppose that these protests were being stirred up by a conspiracy of ice-cream salesmen. After all, they appear to be the only people who are prospering from any of this.

Hmm. The 'Ice-Cream Revolution' certainly has a nice ring to it.

Make mine a fruit sundae with chocolate sprinkles, but easy on the tear gas.

March 2006

Beirut - a nasty run in with a taxi driver

It was almost sunset, as I hailed down an old white Mercedes by the Corniche. "White Tower Hotel?" I asked. "Yes, yes, sit down," the driver instructed. I got into the car and immediately knew I'd made a mistake. The driver's name was Joseph and he was a robust old fella, who looked like he'd survived a few battles in life. "I take you on tour, one hour, fifty dollars, tell you the civil war places," he said. It didn't sound like a question, rather it was more of an instruction. "No, no, just take me to the White Tower Hotel," I explained. He shrugged reluctantly and drove off. "You have a girlfriend?" he asked. "Nice pretty Lebanese students, I know a very good place. Students, good massage..." I declined. Joseph pulled over, not two hundred yards from where he had picked me up. "White Hotel," indicated Joseph. "Uh no," I replied. "I asked for the White Tower Hotel," and thrust the brochure under his grey whiskery nose. His mood soured noticeably. "You tell me tower, many tower hotel here!" We continued the journey. The roads were heavily congested because of the Ramadan rush-hour. Inside, his car is fully reconditioned and looks expensive. He must have got the money somehow. I should have hailed a cheaper looking taxi.

Joseph turned onto a highway. Cars were overtaking relentlessly in every direction. To my surprise, we slowed down and pulled onto the hard shoulder. For a moment, I was wondering what the hell was going on.

And then the penny dropped. Joseph had backed the car up and is about to turn around. "Where are you going?" I asked, but I think I already knew the answer. "Is shortcut. Is too dangerous?" For the first time since being in the Middle East, I was genuinely scared. He was almost about to drive against the oncoming traffic of a three-lane motorway, traffic moving at 70 miles per hour. "Oh no, no!" I tell him, pointing up the road. "That way!" Joseph looked at me with disdain and continued our journey, fortunately on the right side of the road.

We seemed to have been in the cab for an eternity when Joseph finally pulled over, near the hotel. We hadn't arranged a price and there was no meter in the cab, which wasn't entirely unusual. Now, we had to negotiate a price in broken English. I placed 15,000 lire on the dashboard. To say that Joseph was not impressed would be a something of an understatement. He was absolutely bloody furious. "No! Dollar! You give me ten US dollar!" His pale face flushed red with anger. "I don't have any dollars," I explained. "Look, I've taken this journey before and the fare is always 15,000 lire, not ten dollars..." Joseph reached over and grabbed my arm so firmly, it hurt. For an old man, he was strong with a vice-like grip, tensile like an animal.

I was in a complete pickle and I didn't have many options. Looking him in the eye, I firmly told him to let go of my arm. Joseph loosened his grip and I reached for my wallet again. I was almost out of cash, with just a lonely 5,000 lire note sitting in my wallet. I slapped it down on the dash along with the rest of the money, and told him "That's all I have", as I reached for the door handle. Swinging open the door, I grabbed my bag and jumped out of the car.

My heart was beating furiously, as I walked quickly towards the hotel. Behind me, I heard a car door click open. I turned around to see Joseph walking towards me. What else could I do? I sprinted towards the safety of the hotel, and took the steps two at a time without daring to look behind. The hotel reception staff gave me an odd look as

I thumped the elevator button. Fumbling for the bedroom key, I was still nervous. And it's not until I locked my room door behind me that I finally felt safe.

Adrenalin surging, my heart was beating a furious rhythm. I needed to relax, so I ran a bath and enjoyed a long soak. I then sat on the edge of my bed and switched on the television. In all the excitement of the day, I hadn't seen nor heard the news. Every channel was broadcasting the same thing, a coffin being carried towards a large grey aircraft on the shoulders of men in full military uniform. Arafat was dead. It was nothing less than the passing of an era. Perhaps this even explained why Joseph had been so eager to kill us both in a pointless traffic accident. But I doubt it. Aren't taxi drivers like that the world over?

November 2004

Dating in Damascus

Our host in Damascus is Ahmed. A genial and generous doctor, he lays across the marble floor. Stretched out like a sultan in his palace, he dispenses his advice like he dispenses his prescriptions.

"Listen to me," he explains carefully. "Family is very important, but you won't be waking up next to her family every morning."

I should explain that I'm visiting Syria with my old friend, Mark, a British Syrian, who is looking for a wife. It's not an arranged marriage, but still, the dating scene is quite different here.

"Johnny, I met a nice girl yesterday." He pulls out his phone and shows me a photo of a young lovely, fair with golden honey hair. "She's only seventeen, but I don't think this will be a problem. We got on very well." "How long did you see her for?" I asked. "About ten minutes," he said, before adding "Another ten minutes and we might be engaged!"

Further girls are lined up for 4pm, 7pm and 9pm the following day. But the series of events doesn't sound like much fun. It's not like they're going to see a movie and maybe grab a bite to eat. The proceedings are strangely formal, and resemble a business merger much more than a date.

Take the first date; the prospective couple is joined by both sets of parents. In Syria, you are not just marrying the individual, but also entering agreements with their family. Although Mark's family is Christian rather than Islamic, the process of choosing a partner remains more or less the same. Typically the mother orchestrates the meetings, and chooses potential partners from suitable families. The intended and their family are then invited over for tea, and several plates of food. The whole process is somewhat like a job interview, sitting there, drinking tea in your best suit. Constantly on your best behaviour, always careful not to say anything incriminating or foolish in front of your potential in-laws. My friend Mark may decide who to marry, but as always in such situations, the parents have the power of veto too. Mark's mother isn't too keen on the seventeen year old. "She is very nice, but the age gap, it is too much, Mark. She is too young for you to marry, habibi." she explains.

Mark has another date lined up, and this time it is one-on-one, which is usually a good sign. I'm curious as to what he talks about on these dates, so I ask him. "Usual stuff," he says, "life and work, and hopefully we have a laugh. We then talk about marriage, children, the future, that sort of thing." "But it's only a second date!" I remind him, "Surely it's a bit soon to be thinking, let alone talking that far ahead. "Johnny," he explains, "things move quickly out here. I'm not meeting these women just for a bit of boom-badda-boom, I want to get married." "So, you're not interested in the boom-badda-boom?" I ask, knowing Mark well enough. "I'd love some! But that's not how it works out here," he answers, visibly disappointed. "But I've got two weeks to get engaged, before we leave Syria. Then I reckon we can be married by Christmas, then there will be plenty of time for boom-badda-boom!"

Later, during a visit to Hama I strike up a conversation with the hotel manager. "In the west," he explains "first you sleep with a woman, live with her for a while, then you get married, bored and split up. It is all wrong. It is how you say, upside down. Here, in Syria you must first marry a woman, and then you get to know her and fall in love."

His approach might seem like a shocking way of going about getting married in the twenty-first century, but I imagine his attitude wasn't so very different to that of many Brits before the days of bra burnings and the pill. Our attention drifts to the television for a moment. It's tuned to Al-Jazeera Sport, and no, it isn't showing Osama Bin Laden racing camels across the Torra Borra, or jihad netball for that matter. The football is interrupted by adverts, featuring lively men of varying ages who are energetically leaping about their well manicured gardens. They all wear cheery self satisfied grins on their faces. The screen fades and an enthusiastic Arabic voice makes a dramatic announcement, as a blue diamond pill pops up on the screen with a large 'V'. Is this really an advert for Viagra? My new friend looks rather taken aback and admits "Well, times are changing here too."

October 2004

Made in the USA
Las Vegas, NV
13 October 2022